SCALE

Master Opportunities, Avoid Mistakes & Build A Financially Successful Business

AMOL MAHESHWARI

SHWETA JHAJHARIA

WINNER OF 2 INTERNATIONAL STEVIE AWARDS

Re think

First published in Great Britain in 2023
by Rethink Press (www.rethinkpress.com)

© Copyright Amol Maheshwari and Shweta Jhajharia

To our loving parents

Contents

Introduction

If you own or manage a business, one of the most important things you do is make decisions. And the quality of your decisions is among the most important determinants of the success of the business. So how are your decisions informed? What scoreboards and measurable metrics are you looking at to increase the probability of your making better decisions?

Having worked with thousands of business owners, management teams and leaders across the UK, we've realised that businesses do better and sustain improved performance when the leadership team understands how financial success is measured and how different financial metrics impact business performance.

If you feel as though you're always on a rollercoaster of emotions and performance, in business – despite being extremely good at what you do – you're not alone. In fact, you are in the majority of businesses, where the owner and management work tirelessly, till they get tired. Then they rest and work tirelessly again. Unfortunately, as they continue this cycle, they realise they only ever get tired and the quality of life they wanted to create for themselves and for their loved ones when they started seems only to get further away.

Business owners and management teams that understand how to run the 'business' end of the business get real results – and business gets easier every year. They focus on improving their critical business skills to create sustainable financial success. They don't rely on 'lucky breaks' and begin to create a business that continues to improve, sustainably, every year.

This book focuses on some of the fundamental knowledge that will help you do this.

What your business is saying

Most management teams know how to deliver their product or service well but think of themselves as 'non-finance' people and believe that finance is something complicated and best left to bookkeepers and accountants.

For most entrepreneurs, their business is their baby. This baby speaks a different language – the language of numbers. Most business owners and management teams never realise that they need to learn this language. Unfortunately, they are too busy working in the business to spend time doing so and when the business gets a 'bug' they are unable to recognise the symptoms.

Have you ever felt that your team is all over the place with each person driving their own agenda based on what they believe is important to their job?

Have you ever felt worried about paying salaries or the next bill and seen your business as a never-ending treadmill?

Have you ever had that 'Groundhog Day' feeling where today just appears to be a repeat of every day this year? You feel stuck in a glorified job you've created for yourself and can't see the way forward?

These are the 'bugs' afflicting your business and your business is actually telling you exactly what is wrong – in numbers. Unfortunately, you've left the numbers to your accountant to look at once a year! Imagine checking your baby's health once a year!

Understand measures to understand performance

The first step to understanding the language of numbers is to understand what we are aiming to achieve. Then we begin to measure regularly against this aim to calibrate performance. Have you defined the 'health' you want your business to achieve? And are you watching the scorecard regularly?

In *Alice in Wonderland*,[1] Alice asks the Cheshire Cat for directions.

ALICE: Would you tell me, please, which way I ought to go from here?

THE CHESHIRE CAT: That depends a good deal on where you want to get to.

ALICE: I don't much care where.

THE CHESHIRE CAT: Then it doesn't much matter which way you go.

ALICE: ...so long as I get somewhere.

THE CHESHIRE CAT: Oh, you're sure to do that, if only you walk long enough.

Without defined goals for the business, and ways to measure what it is achieving, does it really matter what it does and where it ends up?

Think of these words and phrases: feet wet, deadhead crew, George, jump seat, Zulu time, air pocket, tree, pan-pan. Each of these has a special meaning to a professional pilot. They will not only understand the words, but also know the exact relevance and importance of each one.

Now think of these phrases: working capital, operating leverage, cash gap, debtor days, EBITDA

---

1 Lewis Carroll, *Alice's Adventures in Wonderland* (Macmillan, 1865)

multiple, return on equity and break-even point. These are words that a professional businessperson not only understands, but also applies whenever they make a decision about their business.

Importantly, these are not just words – each is in fact a number. If you want to increase the probability of your success in business, you must become fluent in this language of numbers and know how to apply it directly.

We often hear the excuse that finance is complex and there are other fires to fight without adding more work. Unfortunately, most books on business finance are either too technical or addressed to bigger businesses. This book seeks to fill the gap by creating an easy reference guide that walks through the basic numbers you and everyone in your management team needs to understand, with examples of how that number can be managed and improved to create a financially successful business.

Financial statements are scorecards and, in business, you keep score in money. Without being able to understand your financial statements and differentiate between profits, cash flow and return on investment, how would you know whether you're improving – or even measuring what matters? After working with hundreds of businesses, we have seen business owners and management teams who lack either knowledge or discipline. Understanding your business scorecard is 'non-negotiable'. This book presents that knowledge in an easily digestible format.

Mastery will put you in control

Often business owners 'fall' into their business, by accident or through circumstances – a good idea or a turn of events. They learn how to do the technical work required to offering a good product or service and begin to tell themselves 'I can figure the rest out'. Often, too, they have started at the bottom and risen through successfully delivering what the business offers. Through failing to invest in their own education they rediscover the Peter Principle.[2]

The Peter Principle says organisations tend to promote people to the level at which they become incompetent. People are promoted for being good at what they do. As long as they continue to do a good job in their new role, they keep being promoted. Finally, they reach a place for which they are not suited and stop performing well. They don't get promoted anymore and continue to underperform because they have reached their level of incompetence.

How long does someone take to become a professional? How much work does a plumber, an electrician, a doctor, a solicitor, an accountant have to do and how much must they learn before you trust them? How comfortable would you be, sitting in front of a dentist who still has to keep the textbook open? How confident would you be, wiring your own house after a one-day workshop? Would you call yourself a professional electrician?

---

2   Laurence J Peter and Raymond Hull, *The Peter Principle* (William Morrow and Co., 1969)

Now, think about how many years of experience one needs to become a professional business owner or Managing Director. Unfortunately, in business someone can call themselves an entrepreneur, business owner or Managing Director in less than four minutes – the time it takes to register a business or set up an online profile. The barriers to entry in the profession of business are extremely low. Is it therefore any surprise that the failure rate is so high?

Working with multiple businesses across different sectors, we have realised that understanding financials is key to mastering success in business. Your role as a business leader is to ensure the effective and efficient allocation of resources to maximise long-term returns. Understanding the numbers not only gives you a competitive advantage, but is essential to running a healthy business.

How do you make sure that your decisions are better than flipping a coin? How do you make sure you are not constantly avoiding making decisions or using your 'gut' to guide the business? How much time and money have you really invested in learning this aspect of your profession?

Before you can build your business, you need to build a business foundation. Understanding financial statements and the business's 'score' is a fundamental skill. Understanding the score does not necessarily mean you will make all the right decisions. But the probability of success and higher profitability will increase significantly.

*# Key Principle: Understanding the score is what
drives sustainability in business performance*

Your building blocks to mastery

The fundamentals of a business are basic and uncomplicated. This book aims to demystify the jargon, so you learn to home in on the numbers and ratios that really matter.

To get the most from this book, treat it as an intensive class or series of classes of a college degree. Set reading sessions that work for you and keep your business numbers alongside in each session, for reference and as a case study.

Make notes (on the book, in a notebook, a computer, a phone) so you can revisit concepts as you apply them in your business in future. Treat this as a training course, not a leisure activity. Keep an open and active mindset. Dr Nido Qubein says, 'the price of discipline is always less than the pain of regret'.[3] You have the opportunity to really understand the score. Make sure you give it your best shot.

Applied learning is leveraging knowledge, one of the best forms of leverage in life. You learn once, but apply it again and again. Embrace the learning and enjoy the process of becoming an even better business professional!

---

3   www.nidoqubein.com

The book has three parts.

Part One reviews the basics of the key financial statements – the things that every owner and manager needs to be aware of. These are crucial concepts and numbers that you should have at your fingertips. This part has been structured so you can keep going back to refer to specific concepts you may come across when you look at your own business financials.

Part Two is a case study, to help you create financial statements from scratch for a business. We go right back to the fundamentals – the chassis on which a business is built. This part shows you how to build detailed accounts from how a simple business actually operates and working through it systematically will ensure that you never feel intimidated by financial statements again.

Part Three reviews some key concepts that are often ignored or misunderstood, that underline how management should think about business. We build example scorecards that you could use to summarise the information you need to look at regularly.

PART ONE

THE DEFINITIVE SCORECARDS OF YOUR BUSINESS

1
Your Financial Statements

Your business's financial statements, more than anything else in the business, reveal whether it is a good business with a real and durable advantage or a mediocre business which is likely to continue to return average results.

Before we get into the details of the financial statements, it is important to remember that accounting is both an art and a science. Financial statements are influenced by management estimates and judgements and it is important to be aware of the manner in which you can influence your business financial statements. Given that most countries require businesses to submit regular financial statements, often annual, most businesses draw up full financial accounts only so they can meet that requirement (and so tax can be calculated).

Often, we recommend that businesses maintain a set of management accounts, separate from their financial accounts. These give a clear insight into the real operating performance of the business. Having a set of management accounts means that you can separate out decisions taken for personal or tax reasons (which may affect what financial accounts show) from business decisions.

The core financial statements are the Profit and Loss statement (also referred to as the Income Statement), the Balance Sheet and the Cash Flow statement.

The Profit & Loss (P&L) statement

This statement tells you how much money the business has earned during a stated period. In a well-run business, management will look at the P&L statement every month, if not every week, at a minimum. A final statement is generated once a year – a period referred to as the financial year of the business.

The P&L statement can show crucial information about business margins and the consistency and direction of your earnings.

The Balance Sheet

When a business owner or manager looks at the financial statements for the first time, they go to the P&L statement; but when an investor or outside board member looks at the statements, they usually go to the Balance Sheet first.

The Balance Sheet tells us how much money the business has in the bank and how much money it owes. Subtract the money owed from the money in the bank and we get the net worth of the business. A business can create a balance sheet for any day of the year, which will show what it owns, what it owes and its net worth on that day. In a well-run business, you look at the balance sheet every month (at least) as part of the management accounts, and to ensure that the P&L statement is correct.

If Profit and Loss is like a movie for the business, showing what's happened over a period, the Balance Sheet is a snapshot that shows how the business stands on one date.

> # *Key Principle: The Profit and Loss statement is like a film whereas a Balance Sheet is like a snapshot*

The Cash Flow statement

Most businesses are not required to show a statement of cash flow as part of their financial accounts, and therefore don't, which is a shame as it contains quite a bit of crucial information for managing a business well.

The cash flow statement tracks the cash that flows in and out of the business. It shows how much money the business is spending on capital improvements and tracks movements in debt and equity (terms we explain in Chapter 8).

Notes to the financial statements: hidden treasure

The core financial statements are often summary reports and may not provide enough information for a thorough understanding of the business.

The Notes to the financial statements are where the real detail lies: management and accountants make assumptions about certain things (for example, how long assets will last) and disclose how the firm's position has changed since the previous accounts, and these and other details are given in the Notes.

You need to understand the notes to financial statements in order to properly evaluate a business's financial condition and performance.

Financial ratios and indicators: Your decision-making edge

The bare numbers in financial statements are often not as valuable for analysis as the ratios between two or more figures. There are several well-established ratios and indicators that transform these numbers into meaningful relationships, to allow an in-depth understanding of business financial performance and condition. The power of ratios lies in the fact that the numbers by themselves do not reveal the whole story – the vital question is usually 'compared to what?'

Further, ratios can themselves be compared over time, against projections and against industry averages, to generate powerful insights.

While every industry has a few metrics that are peculiar to it, and businesses at different stages of their growth need to focus on different metrics, the management team in every business should keep a close eye on a few fundamental indicators.

Financial ratios are also a useful tool for spotting differences between reported and actual performance. As an example, sometimes wholesale and distribution businesses allow a customer to buy stock, take delivery but only pay as the stock is sold on to its own customer. This allows you to offer your customer cash flow advantages and lower risk, while still reporting sales (and therefore profitability). A receivable days ratio (explained in Chapter 7) will immediately highlight where this is something the business is doing.

In each chapter to come, we review the key financial ratios and indicators alongside the financial statements and then pull it all together in Part Three. But first, here's a case study we'll return to later in this book.

CASE STUDY: Roger's business

Roger runs a multi-million-pound commercial fit-out business.

He had just been on the phone with a customer, who had decided to delay their job. He had been really counting on the initial payment from the customer, to be able to pay his employees on time this month.

He just could not understand what was happening. His team had never been busier – his focus on high-quality delivery over several years had finally started moving the flywheel and business was pouring in like never before. He had just completed one of his largest projects – on time – and the customer was thrilled how few problems and snags had arisen.

His key furniture supplier, however, had not been paid for over three months while Roger juggled to make sure there was enough cash in the business – he had had to put his own money into the business several times over the year.

Roger had been running his business for over a decade, but still felt out of his depth when issues like this came up. He was beginning to question his own and his business's management capability and wondering whether he should go back to being a much smaller business rather than trying to grow. Then there were the constant stream of letters from people who wanted to buy his business for no money down! Perhaps they would take on these constant cash flow headaches with the business, leaving him to start afresh?

He realised that he needed to call in some expert help and got in touch with Growth Idea, our consulting firm.

The art of finance

Accounting attempts to capture and reflect the reality of the business based on reasonable assumptions and estimates. It builds a map through which to understand the territory – and it is therefore important to always remember that the map is not the territory. Judgements, assumptions, estimates and biases inherent in accounting often make it more an art than a science.

To appreciate and really understand your financial statements in depth, you need to understand some of the rules used to build the statements. The first rule is that many numbers in financial statements reflect assumptions and estimates. A few other rules are presented below.

Accrual vs cash

For businesses with low complexity, income (revenue) can be counted as cash is received and similarly expenses can be counted when cash leaves the business – this is the cash basis of accounting.

For a true picture of the business performance and viability, revenues are recorded when goods or services are delivered (which is usually when your customer becomes liable to pay you for them), irrespective of when actual cash is received from customers, and expenses recorded when incurred (when you become liable to pay them), irrespective of when you pay for these expenses. Because these flows may not coincide with the actual receipt and disbursement of cash this is called accrual accounting. Make sure your business follows accrual accounting and, if it does not, change your accountant and then change to accrual accounting.

> # *Key Principle: Make sure your business accounts use accrual accounting*

The four conventions

So one set of financial statements can reasonably be compared with another, it is useful to have core principles defined for how accounts should be presented. Four key conventions form the basis of most accounts:

1. **Consistency:** Ensuring that assumptions are applied consistently over different periods of time. This ensures that an analysis of financial statements is done on a like-for-like basis.

2. **Conservatism:** Losses are recognised whenever quantifiable and gains are recorded only after they have accrued (see accrual accounting, above). This convention attempts to pre-empt management optimism about the prospects of the business when reporting externally.

3. **Materiality:** Everything significant that affects or has the potential to affect the financial situation of the business is disclosed and, conversely, insignificant items are not separated out.

This allows the statements to focus on items that make a difference rather than striving to perfectly capture every detail.

4. **Full disclosure:** All changes in accounting methods and assumptions are disclosed, especially if they are material. This allows statements to be interpreted with full information about how close they are to depicting the real situation of the business.

The matching principle

This principle requires the financial statements to match revenue and expenses in every period reported – that means all costs associated with the generation of revenue are recorded in that period, even if some are due for payment later or have been paid in advance.

This is an important principle because it separates the physical activity in the business and cash movement from the financial activity recorded in the statements. For this reason it can confuse untrained owners or managers. For example, when a business buys goods to resell over multiple periods, the accounts for each period only record the cost of the goods sold in that period; similarly, when a business buys a machine, the cost of the machine is spread over its expected life.

2

The Profit & Loss Statement: Predictability And Sustainability

The Profit & Loss (P&L) statement summarises business performance over a period. At its core, it records the total sales (or revenue/income) achieved in a period, the expenses over the same period and therefore the profit (or loss) the business has made.

$$Sales - Expenses = Profit$$

The P&L is usually presented in comparison to a previous period, to add immediate additional information on comparative performance and potentially the sustainability of the profits of the business.

The individual components of a business's P&L not only tell you whether the business has made money but also inform on how sustainable the profitability of the business is likely to be, based on how the money has been made. This is a crucial point – the P&L is a commentary on both the actual earnings of the business and the source of these earnings – the latter is often more important, but neglected by those who are unable to understand financial statements. The following table shows what a typical P&L statement looks like; you may want to bookmark this page as reference. We systematically describe the elements of this table in the next three chapters.

Profit & Loss statement

(£ in '000s)	This year	Last year
Turnover	2,000	1,800
Cost of sales	(800)	(750)
Gross profit	1,200	1,050
Administrative expenses		
Marketing expenses	(120)	(120)
Research & development expenses	(100)	(100)
Depreciation	(50)	(50)
Other operating expenses	(500)	(510)
Net operating profit	430	270
Interest expense	(146)	(146)
Other income/expense	9	(5)
Profit before tax	293	119
Tax	(96)	(35)
Profit after tax	**197**	**84**

The next three chapters will focus on each line of this example P&L and delve into how to really understand each of these numbers, to really manage your business.

Key Principle: A P&L summary – sales less
  expenses equals profits

Revenue

The P&L starts with total revenue (sometimes called turnover) and this is therefore also referred to as the top line of the accounts. This is the amount of money that came in the door during the period in question – monthly, quarterly or yearly.

One indicator to look for alongside the revenue number is revenue growth over a similar previous period. This indicates whether the business has been growing or declining over the period measured.

Revenue growth % = (current revenue – previous revenue) ÷ previous revenue %

Key Principle: Revenue is the top line of the
  business

A business having a lot of revenue doesn't mean it is earning a profit. To determine whether a business is earning a profit, you need to deduct the expenses of the business from its net revenues. Net revenue minus expenses equals profit (or loss).

Cost of goods sold

Right underneath revenue on the P&L comes the cost of goods sold. 'Cost of sales' is the equivalent term usually used if the business provides services rather than products.

This cost includes what the business had to pay to purchase the goods or services it sold during the period, the cost of the materials and labour used to manufacture the products it sold in that period and the expenses directly related to the supply of these goods and services. It's important to note that based on accrual accounting, it is not what it spent in that period, rather, what is accrued as costs.

Good businesses try to capture all 'direct' costs in this cost number. This is done by asking the question, if we make another £1,000 of sales, which costs will go up and by how much? Equally, if we sell £1,000 less, which costs would go down and by how much? For sales-led businesses, sales-linked employee incentives are a good example of what should be included in costs of sale.

Clarity on what should be included in calculating the cost of goods sold/cost of sales is important to understand your business well.

 # Key Principle: Review your accounts to ensure all direct costs are captured in cost of sales

Gross profit and gross margin

Subtracting the business's cost of sales from its turnover gives the gross profit. Gross profit is how much of the turnover is left after accounting for the money spent on buying raw material and the direct labour used to make the goods (and any other direct costs included). Because it includes all costs directly related to providing the goods and/or services you offer this makes the gross profit something that every business should monitor on a monthly, if not weekly, basis.

Gross profit is used to calculate the business's gross profit margin, which can tell us a lot about the nature of the business, its core business strategy and its ongoing performance.

Most businesses choose to focus either on a low-cost strategy or one of differentiation. A cost-focused strategy leads to a lower gross margin and, unless the business continues to scale and benefit from economies, a business model that is unsustainable in the long term. A higher gross margin allows for pricing flexibility and significant competitive advantages.

> # *Key Principle: Differentiate your products and services to increase gross margin*

Administrative expenses

Beneath the gross profit line on the P&L, all other expenses are usually consolidated into the administrative expense category. This is usually a 'catch-all' category, so hides a lot of information that the management team needs to separate out to understand the performance of the business. It is important for management to be able to dive into each line item on a regular basis, so they can properly budget and analyse variances in performance and costs.

All the business's indirect costs should be found here: those associated with research and development of new products, marketing and selling, administrative aspects of getting the goods or services to market, depreciation and amortisation, restructuring and impairment charges, employee costs and the catch-all 'other'. This often includes non-operating, non-recurring expenses, too. When these entries are added, they make up the total administrative expenses, which are then subtracted from the gross profit to arrive at the business's operating profit or loss.

The example here separates administrative expenses into four groups: marketing, R&D, depreciation and other operating expenses. This has been done for explanatory purposes, to focus on some key items to look for when reviewing business performance. Your business might need other lines, for example for employee expenses or rental and lease charges especially if these account for a significant portion of administrative expenses.

Net operating profit and operating profit margin

Subtracting the business's administrative expenses from its gross profit gives us the net operating profit (or operating income). This is how much of the revenue remains after accounting for all money spent on operating the business – both direct and indirect. If non-operating income and expenses have been correctly separated out, the net operating profit and the operating profit margin are key indicators of the performance and viability of the business.

> # Key Principle: Operating profit margin is the
> metric that differentiates winners in business

There are significant opportunity costs for the business owner associated with choosing to run their own business and one major one is the capital invested in the business. The operating profit can be used to compare the business to other opportunities available to the business owner, to understand whether continuing to deploy current and/or future capital in the business remains a good decision.

We will explore the use of operating profit to understand returns on assets and capital in Chapter 17.

Interest expense and interest income

Interest expense is the interest payable on the debt owed by the business. As it is a financial cost, not an operating one, it is reported separately. As we will note in Chapter 6, the decision whether to finance a business with equity or debt is a separate one from decisions about operating the business and the effects of this decision therefore need to be separated out for analysis, rather than obscuring the analysis of operating performance.

Sometimes there may be a separate line for financial/interest income earned, but given that most businesses earn little in interest, we have chosen to show a combined interest expense/income line.

 # Key Principle: The P&L reflects both operating and financial decisions made by the business

Other income/expense

A business may have other sources of income which are not strictly related to the business.

These may be one-time – for example, when a business sells a 'non-current' asset (see Chapter 7), the profit or loss for the sale is recorded as other income. The profit or loss is the difference between the proceeds from the sale and the value originally stated in historical business accounts, after depreciation.

This is also where non-operating, unusual and infrequent income and expense events are reported in the P&L. Common types of income include income from investments, rents and grants and common types of expense include discretionary expenditures (usually incurred by the owner) and non-recurring events, and either of these can significantly affect a business's overall profitability. Since these are non-recurring events, they should be clearly, separately identified so they can be removed from any calculation of business profitability in determining the true operating performance of the business.

Profit before tax

Profit before tax is a business's income after all expenses have been deducted, but before tax has been subtracted. This number is perhaps the most relevant when trying to understand the return that the business is earning.

If a business owner has £1 million invested in her business and is making a pre-tax return of £50,000, she needs to compare this to what she would make if she invested the same amount in another opportunity, to understand whether it is worthwhile to continue to work hard in the business when benchmarked against, say investing in the stock markets or in property.

Looking at profit in pre-tax terms enables a business owner to think about a business or investment in terms that can be compared to other investments.

Tax

Taxes payable are recorded on the P&L under the tax heading.

Corporation/business taxes are based on tax accounts (accounts that have to be prepared using governmental tax guidelines), not on financial accounts. This is a separate set of accounts that your accountant prepares every year to calculate tax due. These often adjust for tax credits and discretionary spending by the owner and may not exactly reflect the profit before tax shown on the financial statements. Importantly, some items (e.g. capital expenses and depreciation) may be treated differently in the tax and financial accounts.

> # *Key Principle: Tax accounts and management accounts need to be distinct*

Profit after tax

After all the expenses and taxes have been deducted from a business's revenue, we get the profit after tax, also called the 'bottom line' of the business. This is the amount that the business owner can either retain and reinvest in the business or choose to take out as dividends.

3
Revenue, Profit And Margin

Revenue: Avoiding the top-line trap

For businesses selling multiple products and services across several countries, the management accounts should break down which department, product, service or geography contributes the revenue, to get a true understanding of how the top line is made up. Combining everything into one 'Sales' line risks losing material information on where the real money in the business is being made.

Here's an example of a business where purely looking at the top line is likely to be insufficient for a proper understanding of how the business is performing:

Revenue analysis	Current year	Previous year
Service A	£1,200,000	£1,500,000
Service B	£600,000	£300,000
Product C	£200,000	£200,000
Total revenue	£2,000,000	£2,000,000

The total revenue figure hides tremendous volatility in two of the services that the business provides. While Service A has been declining, Service B has doubled.

As not all revenue is equal, the next question to ask would be which of these revenue streams is better. Sustainable or recurring revenue is a lot more valuable for a business. If Service B is a recurring service (for example, ongoing support services) whereas Service A is one-off (for example, project-based/installation services), the business has actually done well in the current year.

Key Principle: Not all revenue is created equal.
   Recurring revenue is precious

Further, deeper analysis of revenue would look at the components of the services themselves.

Revenue = customers × average £ value of
each transaction × number of transactions

Revenue analysis Product C	Current year	Previous year
Customers	125	100
Average £ value	£200	£200
Transactions	8	10
Revenue	125 × £200 × 8 = £200,000	100 × £200 × 10 = £200,000

Looking through the above numbers, it seems that while the number of customers has increased by 25%, each customer is only coming back eight times instead of ten (a 20% decrease). The business needs to start focusing on repeat custom and at the same time start thinking of increasing their pricing.

This analysis also yields another key insight into how revenue works. A decrease in any component of revenue requires a lot of effort by other components for the business just to stay in the same place! This is a crucial lesson when thinking of discounting prices (decreasing average £ value) – the increase in customers required is likely to be higher than you think. To work with the numbers above,

Revenue analysis Product C	Next year	Current year	Previous year
Customers	125	125	100
Average £ value	£160	£200	£200
Transactions	10	8	10
Revenue	125 × £160 × 10 = £200,000	125 × £200 × 8 = £200,000	100 × £200 × 10 = £200,000

If the business decides to drop its prices by 20% (for example by offering the fifth product free to every customer), to get customers to come back more, the number of transactions would need to return to its previous levels (the same number of customers, but 25% more transactions) to maintain revenue at the same level. And this effect is exacerbated when the product has a lower margin.

Key Principle: Think hard before discounting

It is important to remember that management, alongside the accountant, decide what revenue is recognised on the accounts – and this can increase pressure to massage the numbers. Judgements on what revenue should be recognised in a period could be required when the revenue will only come in once a project is completed, so management needs to estimate when that will be. Similarly, software providers may sometimes recognise revenue up front even though the fees will be collected at stages, or over multiple periods of time.

The estimation and relative fluidity that revenue recognition affords has meant that it is often implicated in accounting frauds – some that have even sounded the death knell of accounting firms and businesses – Arthur Andersen and Enron!

Key Principle: Revenue recognition is based on judgement

Remember that the revenue captured in the financial statements is always net of sales tax (if any) and Value Added Tax, which has only been collected on behalf of the government and does not belong to the business. Assuming that incoming cash (which includes tax) equals revenue can have disastrous implications for the cash flow of the business.

Value Added or sales tax should not show on the P&L statement of the business or in any operating analysis. It is not included in the 'Tax' line, which records tax on the business's profits. Some management teams have made the mistake of assuming stellar performance when looking at gross revenue, only to find to their surprise that their financial statements show extremely low profitability and the business struggles for cash every time payments have to be made.

Cost of goods sold: Common mistakes that shroud reality

A simple example of how a furniture trading business might calculate its cost of goods would be:

$$\text{Cost of goods sold} = \text{beginning inventory} + \text{purchases} - \text{ending inventory}$$

If the business starts the year with £900,000 in inventory, makes £400,000 in purchases to add to the inventory, and ends the period with an inventory value of £500,000, the business's cost of goods for the period would be £800,000.

If the business instead purchases raw material to make and install furniture, its cost of goods would be:

Cost of goods sold = beginning raw material + purchases − ending raw material + cost of labour

While accountants are quite adept at recording purchases and sales, often they rely on the business to report the value of inventory. This unfortunately means that sometimes the business ends up completely mis-estimating profitability for most of the year until the actual inventory is reconciled to prepare the accounts at the end of the year, because it takes purchases (of raw material or stock) to be equivalent to cost of goods sold, without reference to how much the inventory has increased or decreased over the period. When inventory levels don't change dramatically, this approach can still give a fair assessment of performance. Unfortunately, it completely fails exactly when this failure begins to matter − when inventory levels start to vary from 'the usual level'.

It is crucial to remember to adjust the amount spent on raw material or stock purchases for the amount by which inventory levels have changed, because in this case the increase in spending might not affect profitability as you expect it to.

> # Key Principle: Ensure your business adjusts the
> P&L for inventory changes regularly

Remember that what is almost always recorded for material and inventory is the historical costs of purchase (what you paid at the time you purchased, whenever that was) – different businesses, and perhaps even different product lines, may use different approaches to filling orders (first in first out, last in first out, weighted average) and this can materially affect the cost of goods sold and therefore the profitability of the business.

For a business, buying in bulk and timing buying decisions is often a key strategy to reduce cost of goods sold. Bulk buying may, however, lead to a false economy because the costs of storage and depletion are hidden away in the administrative expenses (see Chapter 4).

Gross profit and gross margin: The key indicators of competitive advantage

Gross profit is the profit you make after subtracting direct costs from revenue.

Gross profit margin % = gross profit ÷ turnover

If we use the figures in the example P&L statement in Chapter 2, gross profit margin = £1,200 ÷ £2,000 = 60%.

Without a competitive advantage, businesses must compete by lowering the price of the product or service they are selling. That drop, of course, lowers their profit margins and therefore their profitability.

As a rule, businesses need to ensure their gross profit margins are 40% or better. Businesses with gross profit margins below 40% tend to be in highly competitive industries, where competition is hurting overall profit margins. Businesses with gross profit margins of 20% are usually in a fiercely competitive industry. If this is the industry and market you find yourself in, you really need to question whether you could be spending the same effort elsewhere for better results, as the business is likely to remain relatively difficult to continue to run.

Even where it enjoys a high gross profit margin, a business may still have poor performance if administrative costs are high. Most accounts do not really separate the various types of administrative costs in the main accounts (they do this in the trading P&L account at the end of the financial statements). It is important to differentiate the different kinds of costs to enable intelligent decision-making. This is what we seek to do in Chapter 4.

An eye-watering error

Often businesses set the price for their customers using the cost of the stock they have purchased to sell on or of the raw materials purchased – essentially 'cost plus' pricing. This tends to ignore the price that customers might be willing to pay for a high-value product or service.

From a financial perspective, one type of numerical mistake often costs the business a lot more than any other – and that is the habit of confusing mark-ups with margins.

Mark-up is applied to the cost of goods sold: marked-up price = cost of goods sold × (1 + mark-up%).

To use a simple example, if the business constructs kitchens for their customers, they may price in this way:

Material to be used:	£25,000
Sub-contractor costs:	£15,000
Expenses and other charges:	£10,000
Total costs of sales:	£50,000
Mark-up at 20%:	£50,000 × 20% = £10,000
Total price to customer:	£60,000

The equation for calculating gross margin is:

$$\text{Gross margin\%} = (\text{sales} - \text{cost of goods}) \div \text{sales}$$
$$= \text{gross profit} \div \text{sales}$$

Let's now calculate the gross margin in the above example.

$$\text{Gross profit} = \text{sales} - \text{cost of sales}$$
$$= £60,000 - £50,000 = £10,000$$

$$\text{Gross margin\%} = \text{gross profit} \div \text{turnover}$$
$$= £10,000 \div £60,000 = 16.67\%$$

While you might be thinking that you are making 20% because that is the mark-up you apply, you will only be making 16.67% and possibly wondering why the accounts never seem to show you earning the kind of money you feel you should be!

> # *Key Principle: Ensure your pricing is based on gross margins*

Operating profit and operating margin: Was it worth it?

Operating profit is the profit you make after subtracting operating costs from the gross profit. This is the true indicator of whether the business has had a good year. It puts all operating decisions together – decisions that reflect in the reduced or increased expenses through the year. It is also before non-operating income and expenses and focuses on the pure operating performance of the business.

One indicator to look for alongside the operating profit number is operating profit growth over a similar previous period. This indicates whether the business has been growing or declining in profitability over the period measured.

Operating profit growth %
= (current operating profit − previous operating profit)
÷ previous operating profit %

Measured alongside the revenue growth %, the operating profit growth % tells you whether the effort being spent on growing sales is translating to better profitability. For most businesses, costs grow slower than revenue and therefore operating profit growth outstrips revenue growth. If this is not happening, it is likely that management has been ignoring profitability in the pursuit of a higher top line.

$$\text{Operating profit margin \%}$$
$$= \text{operating profit} \div \text{turnover}$$

If we use the figures in the example P&L statement in Chapter 2, operating profit margin = £430 ÷ £2,000 = 21.5%.

Within an industry and among your competitors, comparing the operating margin is perhaps the most useful in indicating how well the business is being run.

In the example the gross profit margin is 60%, and after expenses the operating profit margin is 21.5%. Comparing these two margins tells you important things about how well your business is controlling its indirect costs and expenses. It also gives an indication of the operating leverage built into the business. A large difference between these two numbers indicates a high level of operating leverage in the business which means that small changes in sales are likely to have a large effect on the operating profit of the business. This is covered in more detail in Chapter 18.

Net profit and net margin: The bottom line

The final profitability indicator to look at is the net profit margin.

Net profit margin % = profit after tax ÷ turnover

The net profit margin indicates how much of the work done in getting revenue has translated into the bottom line of the business. Given the choice between running two businesses, one with a revenue of £2 million and another with a revenue of £10 million, which would you choose? But if we tell you that each return a profit after tax of £200,000, you can see that the smaller business is likely to be stronger.

Net margins over 20%, consistently achieved, indicate good businesses. Equally, consistent net margins below 10% indicate that a business is operating in a highly competitive sector in which it is unable to differentiate itself (except for financial businesses, where a low net margin may indicate poor risk management).

As net profit is the money that the business owner can either retain in the business or choose to take out as dividend, the sensible owner will compare the net profit against the capital personally invested in the business. We will do this when we come to analyse the balance sheet, in Chapter 7.

4

Administrative Expenses: Every Line Matters

Operating and non-operating expenses

Administrative expenses should only really include operating costs to give a true indication of how the business operates. For a lot of business owners, personal expenses and decisions are intertwined with their business and this makes it more difficult to analyse the true operating performance of the business.

An important criterion to look at when examining these expenses is how discretionary they are – to what extent the decision to spend the money was based on a business requirement vs what the business owner wanted to do for semi-personal reasons.

Here's an example to illustrate the point. A business owner once added a line for RRV expenses into their accounts. The RRV was a vehicle the business apparently used to make urgent deliveries to customers – when they could not afford to get stuck in traffic. It just so happened that the RRV, or rapid response vehicle, was a gleaming Harley-Davidson which only the owner and his son were allowed to ride – and they did not really do much delivery work. This would perhaps be a strong case for treating the expense as discretionary and non-operating when looking at the performance of the business.

Expenses like director pension contributions, director salary and entertainment expenses are often discretionary costs and should be classified as non-operating if analysis of business performance is to be like-for-like over different periods. For most business owners, having the business pay into their pension is a valuable tax strategy available to them and they can to some extent use these contributions to influence the results the business shows, which is not a problem if the management team does not lose sight of actual performance.

Key Principle: Separate out non-operating and discretionary costs in your accounts

Marketing expenses (or investment?)

When analysing expenses, if the benefits accrue over a longer period of time, they should be considered as investments rather than expenses for the purpose of decision-making, even if the accounts treat them as expenses. Marketing expense is a prime example of this.

While the rule in general is to try and reduce or avoid most expenses, marketing expenses are closely related to the sales a business can achieve. As such, for savvy management teams, marketing is always an investment rather than an expense. Where the management team has a good understanding of their customer acquisition costs for each marketing channel and the lifetime value of each of their customers, they can in fact create an unlimited marketing budget for their business.

As an example, consider the business below, in which two marketing channels (for example, advertising and search engine optimisation) are used every month; for one the marketing expense is £1,000 and for the other the business spends £800. Measuring the enquiries received from each of these channels and the conversion rate of these enquiries, you can calculate the acquisition cost from each channel.

Customer acquisition cost	Channel 1	Channel 2
Marketing spend (monthly)	£1,000	£800
Enquiries	10	8
Conversion rate	20%	25%
New customers (each month)	2	2
Customer acquisition cost	£500	£400

If we now look at what each customer spends with the business, what the business makes from each customer (in gross profit) and understand how long customers continue to work with the business, we can get a good understanding of the lifetime value of each customer.[4]

Lifetime value (LTV) of a customer
= annual spend × gross margin × customer retention

Working through this example, customers acquired from one marketing channel spend £1,200 whereas those acquired from the other spend £1,800 every year – buying different products and services. The LTV of a customer from one channel is therefore £420 whereas from the other channel it is £1,080:

Lifetime value of customer	Channel 1	Channel 2
Customer annual spend	£1,200	£1,800
Average gross margin	35%	40%
Gross profit per customer	£420	£720
Customer average retention (years)	1	1.5
Profit per customer (total)	£420	£1,080

Looking at the numbers above, Channel 1 is not really working for the business. They spend £500 to get a new customer who ends up only increasing profit by £420 – essentially, they are losing £80 for every

4   Shweta Jhajharia, *Sparks: Ideas to ignite your business growth* (Panoma Press, 2017)

customer that this channel brings. You would be well advised to stop spending any money on this channel.

Channel 2 on the other hand has created an unlimited marketing budget for the business. For every £400 spent to bring a new customer in, profitability goes up by £1,080. How much should the business spend on this marketing channel? Perhaps as much as cash flow allows and, in fact, you should seriously consider taking on bank loans to increase marketing expenses here.

> \# *Key Principle: Marketing is classified as an expense in accounts although good marketing is almost always an investment*

Research and development expenses

When a business requires consistent, significant investments in research and development (R&D), innovation and product development, it may be making a lot of money now, but the sustainability of this profitability becomes suspect and it should begin to plan for diversifying the retained profits into other avenues.

If a competitive advantage is created by a patent, as with pharmaceutical businesses, at some point that patent will expire. If the competitive advantage is the result of some technological advancement, there is always the threat that newer technology will replace it. While hardly any industry is completely protected from disruption, businesses with high R&D

expenses are usually in industries more prone to push businesses into distress.

Not only must these businesses spend huge sums of money on R&D, but because they are constantly having to invent new products they must also redesign and update their sales programmes, which means that they also must spend heavily on administration.

A business that does not rely on R&D and constant innovation to stay ahead of the game does not have the constant worry of whether their business would wither away the moment they stop investing and a consistent question mark over the long-term viability of their business.

Depreciation and amortisation

All equipment, machinery and buildings eventually wear out over time and need replacing. This wearing out is recognised on the P&L as depreciation. Essentially, the annual depreciation is an allocation towards the replacement cost of the depreciating asset and the amount by which the asset depreciated can be said to have been used in the business activity of the year.

As an example, take a cutting machine bought by a business for £1 million, which is likely to last for ten years. A business accountant will therefore depreciate the asset over its expected life, allocating £100,000 to expenses in each of the next ten years.

Depreciation is a real cost of doing business, because at some time in the future, the cutting machine will have to be replaced. By allowing an expense for it every year, the business records the value of the asset as decreasing over its ten-year life. In the second year, the asset will show in the Balance Sheet (see Chapter 6) as worth £900,000, then £800,000 in the third year and so on till it shows as £0 at the end of the ten-year period. But over this period, you should have reserved £100,000 of business profit every year so that you have £1 million at the end of it, with which to replace the machine with a new one.

This treatment leads some managers to the fallacy that depreciation is not a 'real' expense. Once the cutting machine is bought and paid for, no more cash outlays need to be made but it does decrease annual profit by the £100,000 yearly depreciation expense for the next ten years. This means that, from a short-term perspective, the business has a yearly cost that isn't actually going out in cash – but, of course, it had to buy the cutting machine at some point in the past and it may have to buy another at some point in the future.

Key Principle: Depreciation may be a 'non-cash' expense but it is still a real expense

Like physical assets, when value is attached to an intangible asset that is depreciating in value (a patent is an example of an intangible asset), its value in the accounts is reduced every year. This reduction in value is called amortisation to indicate that it refers to an intangible asset rather than a physical one. Amortisation, like depreciation, is accumulated on the Balance Sheet to gradually run down the value of the intangible asset.

Sometimes, people valuing businesses add depreciation and amortisation cost back into earnings – to arrive at a revised earnings calculation: EBITDA, meaning earnings before income tax, depreciation and amortisation. EBITDA ignores the fact that eventually the asset, in this case the cutting machine, will wear out and the business will have to come up with another £1 million to buy a new one; and it may not have the cash at that time. Depreciation is a real expense and should always be included in any calculation of earnings. To do otherwise would be to delude ourselves over the short term into believing that the business is earning more than it actually is.

Key Principle: Depreciation is a 'replacement'
expense

If, as a percentage of gross profit, depreciation costs are less than 10%, this indicates a strong business which does not require a lot of investment to maintain profitability.

There is one additional hidden point in the above example. Who decides that the cutting machine is going to last for ten years and not five or fifteen? The choice of the depreciation/amortisation period is important because it impacts the business's profitability quite significantly. While there are some general accounting rules for most assets, the final decision is always a management policy – in essence, the management team decides. And, with enough justification, occasionally the management team can change the depreciation policy.

It is therefore possible to show higher profitability by simply choosing to depreciate assets over as long a period as practical, something that an owner may consider when beginning to plan to value and sell the business. Unless tax calculations use depreciation policies laid down by government regulation, a decision on the period over which to depreciate assets would also change the taxes paid by the business.

> # *Key Principle: Understand the assumptions*
> *behind your depreciation policy*

Other operating expenses

Administrative expenses include management salaries, advertising, travel costs, rent and rates, legal fees, commissions and all payroll costs. As a percentage of sales, they vary greatly from business to business. A good indication of the strength of the business is the extent to which these expenses vary from one year to the next and whether they are trending upwards or downwards.

As administrative expenses are often 'fixed' in nature, businesses with high expenses often find themselves struggling in periods when sales take a hit. Equally, profitability can increase significantly if they can maintain costs when sales increase.

Most good service-based businesses look to keep their administrative costs at around 30% to 60% of their sales, with the bulk of the costs devoted to employee costs. For product-based businesses, often a better comparative metric is to assume 20%–30% of the gross profit will be operating profit.

Interest expense and interest income

With a few exceptions, businesses in competitive industries usually require large capital expenditures to finance assets or working capital or both, so interest payments may be high relative to operating income. Other businesses in this position may have bought property for use as offices, warehouses or industrial units instead of leasing it, and in such cases, the debt may indicate that the business owner has taken a non-operating decision based on personal circumstances. A few people deliberately leverage their business to release dividends for themselves, a strategy that has been used effectively by several successful business owners and is often also pursued by private equity firms.

The ratio of interest payments to operating income can tell you the level of economic risk the business has chosen to take. Often, businesses which are in a high growth phase choose to fund this growth with debt. The debt, and therefore the interest paid by the business, may also reflect the personal financial and risk profile of the business owner and management team and whether they are comfortable with debt or seek to avoid it.

5
A Few Key Concepts

Break-even, contribution
and price competitiveness

As seen in the P&L statement, a business has operating costs that are usually incurred irrespective of whether the business makes more or less sales. So, the initial sales and gross profit a business makes are needed just to cover these fixed operating expenses. The business only makes an operating profit once it makes more sales than this point at which gross profit exceeds operating costs. This is referred to as the break-even point of the business. At the break-even point, the business is neither making nor losing money.

By establishing the break-even point of your business, you can make informed decisions,[5] such as determining the selling price of your products or services, working out whether a new product line will be profitable or calculating whether it would be profitable to expand the size of your operating facility.

For the purpose of calculating the break-even point, expenses are divided into variable and fixed costs. For most businesses, cost of goods sold/ cost of sales is a good proxy for variable costs whereas administrative expenses are a good proxy for fixed costs. But this may not always be the case, as financial statements do not usually distinguish between fixed and variable costs.

To further complicate matters, some costs may have both fixed and variable elements to them. For example, utility charges relating to a business's administrative offices generally do not vary with the level of sales, though the cost of fuel for running manufacturing equipment could be affected by the number of orders.

Sales less variable costs is referred to as 'contribution', as this is the contribution each sale over the break-even point makes to the bottom line of the business.

Key Principle: Contribution = sales − variable costs

---

5 Contact growthidea.co.uk for a template to help you work out your break-even point.

At the break-even point,

Sales − variable costs = contribution = fixed costs

and break-even sales × contribution margin will exactly equal fixed costs. Hence,

Break-even sales
= fixed costs ÷ contribution margin
= fixed costs ÷ [(sales − variable costs) ÷ sales]

If we use the figures in the example P&L statement in Chapter 2, and assume operating expenses are all fixed whereas costs of goods sold are all variable, this formula simplifies to:

Break-even sales
= operating expenses ÷ gross margin %
= (£120 + £100 + £50 + £500) ÷ 60% = £1,283.33

Remember, the P&L statement shows figures rounded to £'000, so the break-even point is actually £1,283,333.

Further, if we know that each unit of sale is worth £200, we can also calculate that 6,417 units will achieve break-even.

Break-even sales (units)
= break-even sales ÷ average unit sale

The break-even point is often a good line in the sand, to mark when the business stops covering costs and makes profit. In this example, a business might express its minimum target as £3,516 or 17.5 units per day before any team incentives are accrued (assuming sales is spread over 365 days). If sales only happen on working days, you could use the working days in the year (approximately 260) to arrive at the daily sales target for the sales team.

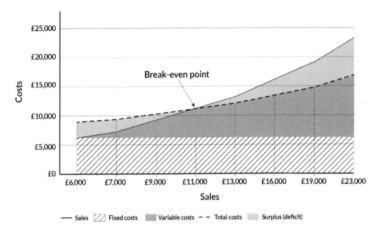

Break-even analysis

In the figure, before the break-even point, costs are higher than sales and the business makes a loss. Once sales have passed the break-even point, every extra sale not only increases the profit the business makes, but also its profit margin.

For a business or product/service in its initial years, break-even sales are also an indicator of viability.

A key reason to understand the break-even of a business is because once break-even sales are achieved, every additional sale makes a contribution directly to the bottom line. This means that once the business has passed this crucial milestone, flexibility in pricing increases – the business can price more competitively because every additional sale adds value to the bottom line.

> *# Key Principle: Think marginal pricing after sales pass break-even*

Tax: The second set of statements

As mentioned in Chapter 2, tax accounts may not exactly reflect the profit before tax shown on the financial statements. Often the tax payable is an indicator of the tax strategies being deployed by the business and how effective these are.

$$\text{Tax payable } \% = \text{tax} \div \text{profit before tax}$$

Importantly, some items (e.g. depreciation) may be treated differently in the tax and financial accounts. Comparing the tax payable % as shown in the financial accounts with the government's published business tax rates could be valuable in suggesting tax-friendly strategies for the business.

Given that tax is a legitimate cost of business, it is important for management to be fully aware of the expenses that *are* allowed for tax purposes and those that *are not*. Where taxes on expenses paid can be claimed back, as is the case with setoffs of Value

Added Tax, inability to ensure tax is being correctly calculated on every expense item could lead to unnecessary losses for the business.

> # *Key Principle: Tax accounts and management accounts need to be distinct*

Often, business owners and management assume that because tax is a specialist subject, they have no ability to influence the tax paid by the business once the year's profits are established. Tax is one of the largest expense items for most businesses and therefore it is important that the business owner and management team always pursue questions around what can be done by the business within the law, to reduce the tax paid.

You don't need to be an expert in tax – you just need to be able to ask your accountant and tax adviser the right questions, to guide your tax expense lower. Reviewing tax expense is perhaps the one place where you look to reduce the profit in the business as this usually directly leads to lower tax expenses. Some of these questions are:

- Are there any investments that the business has made or can make that would carry favourable tax treatment?

- Are the depreciation policies applied across assets tax-efficient or do they need to change?

- How do different types of expense that the business has accrued need to be accounted for?

- Has any income been received in advance that should not be booked as revenue?

- Are there ways to use business funds prior to the end of the year that would attract tax deductions, for example payments into pension funds?

- Do directors / owners incur expenses that could be allocated to the business, for example the cost of using a home office for remote working?

- Are there any provisions that the business needs to make for potential bad debts or future expected losses?

- Has a revaluation or reduction in inventory occurred that needs to be recorded in the accounts?

  # *Key Principle: Tax is one of the largest expenses for most businesses. It deserves management thinking time*

Profit after tax and net margin: The danger of oversimplification

After all the expenses and taxes have been deducted from a business's revenue, we get the profit after tax, also called the 'bottom line' of the business.

One indicator to look for alongside the profit after tax number is growth over a previous similar period. This indicates whether the business profitability has been growing or declining over the period measured.

Growth %

= (current profit − previous profit) ÷ previous profit %

Chapter 3 included an example of a business where looking just at the top line could be seriously misleading; here is the same example, but looking at the bottom line:

Profitability analysis	Current year	Previous year
Service A	£117,000	£147,000
Service B	£60,000	£30,000
Product C	£20,000	£20,000
Total profit after tax	£197,000	£197,000

In this example, overall profitability has remained the same, but the composition has altered materially. Profits from Service B have doubled whereas from Service A they have reduced. You could use this information to ask deeper questions and decide on the future strategy of the business. As mentioned in Chapter 3, not all profits are equal – recurring profits are a lot more valuable for a business. Even with the same overall profitability, the business may actually be better or worse off in the current year.

Consistent profits are usually a sign that the business is selling a product or service that does not need to go through the expensive process of change. An upward trend in profits means that the business is strong enough to allow it either to make the expenditures to increase market share through advertising or expansion, or to pay dividends to the business owner.

Businesses with erratic profitability showing a downward trend are often in industries prone to booms and busts. When demand is greater than supply, they increase production to meet it, which increases costs and can eventually lead to over-supply in the industry. Over-supply drives prices down, and the business starts to lose money until the next economic boom comes along.

6

The Balance Sheet: Making Operating And Financial Decisions

E very business's balance sheet is made up of assets, liabilities and equity. Assets represent things of value that a business owns and has in its possession or that will be received and can be measured objectively. Liabilities are what a business owes to others – creditors, suppliers, tax authorities, employees, etc. They are obligations the business needs to fulfil. Equity represents retained earnings and funds contributed by the business's shareholders, who have accepted the ownership risk in exchange for potential return on their investment. The following table shows what a typical balance sheet looks like; you may want to bookmark this page as reference. We systematically describe the elements of this table in the next three chapters.

Assets	This year (£)	Last year (£)
Property, plant & equipment	2,732,000	2,893,000
Goodwill & intangibles	50,000	50,000
Other long-term assets	0	0
Total non-current assets	**2,782,000**	**2,943,000**
Cash and cash equivalents	1,500	1,700
Inventory	200,000	240,000
Receivables	258,000	185,000
Other current assets	10,000	8,000
Total current assets	**469,500**	**434,700**
Liabilities		
Payables	110,000	130,000
Accrued expenses	24,000	28,000
Other current liabilities	0	0
Total current liabilities	134,000	158,000
Net current assets (liabilities)	**335,500**	**276,700**
Long-term debt	2,629,000	2,892,000
Other long-term liabilities	20,000	15,000
Total non-current liabilities	**2,649,000**	**2,907,000**
Net assets	468,500	312,700
Equity		
Share capital	100,000	100,000
Retained earnings	368,500	212,700
Total equity	**468,500**	**312,700**

The relationship of these items is expressed in the fundamental balance sheet equation:

$$\text{Assets} - \text{liabilities} = \text{equity}$$

You could also turn the equation around to separate the operating and financing parts of the business and for insights into how the assets of the business are financed.

$$\text{Assets} = \text{liabilities} + \text{equity}$$

Using the numbers in the example balance sheet,

Assets   = non-current assets + total current assets

      = £2,782,000 + £469,500 = £3,251,500

Liabilities = total non-current liabilities + total current liabilities

      = £2,649,000 + £134,000 = £2,783,000

Equity   = £3,251,500 − £2,783,000 = £468,500

or viewed the other way round,

£3,251,500 = £2,783,000 + £468,500

Assets less liabilities is often referred to as net assets, and used to mean the 'net' investment by shareholders in the business. Equity is what is often referred to as the net worth of the business. The relationship above therefore can also be expressed as:

Net assets = net worth

 # Key Principle: Assets − liabilities = equity

One of the reasons this relationship is fundamental is that it depicts the decisions the management team is taking – both operating decisions on how to run the business and financing decisions on whether to take external loans or use their own funds to finance the business.

Usually, a business that is growing in sales finds that it also needs a growing asset base – higher levels of inventory, receivables and equipment. Once the business needs more assets, it needs to finance these assets and so it requires either external finance, reinvestment of profits or the business owner to add more funds to it. The 'balance' in 'Balance Sheet' is supposed to tell you that all assets in the business need to be financed by corresponding amounts of liabilities and equity. How assets are supported, or financed, by payables, debt and equity, reveals a lot about a business's financial health and sustainability and also often about the management's comfort with debt.

 # Key Principle: The Balance Sheet always balances

Just as sales growth needs a growing assets base, some businesses choose to grow their asset base through aggressive debt, as this might in turn increase sales. Sometimes potential growth can be unlocked by taking on more leverage; but conversely, sometimes all a business needs to achieve stability is to reduce debt levels by increasing equity.

Unlike the P&L, a Balance Sheet is a snapshot at a point in time. It is usually drawn up at the end of the financial quarter or financial year – and refers to the business's position as on that date.

Both assets and liabilities are divided into current and non-current (we describe these in Chapter 7). In general, assets that are expected to convert to cash within twelve months or sooner are categorised as current assets and liabilities which are expected to be paid within twelve months or sooner are categorised as current liabilities.

Chapters 7, 8 and 9 dive deeper into each of these fundamental elements – assets, liabilities and equity.

Business accounts detail the components that make up assets and liabilities in the 'notes' to the accounts and sometimes the balance sheet presented will be a summary. It is therefore important to look through the notes to the accounts when analysing business performance.

7
Assets

Assets comprise everything that the business owns and include cash, machinery, buildings, patents and amounts owed by other people and businesses to your business.

Assets are usually presented as 'fixed' or 'non-current' assets, and current assets. Fixed or non-current assets in general will not be assets that the business plans to convert to cash for its ongoing operational requirements; current assets are everything that is either cash or can be converted to cash within a short period (usually within a year). They indicate the amount that will be quickly accessible to the business in case of emergency requirements.

A really important accounting convention to remember when looking at the Balance Sheet of any business is that most assets will be shown at historical value (the price when they were acquired) and adjusted for depreciation that has been charged against them since they were acquired. This may by now have little to do with current value.

> # *Key Principle: Assets in the Balance Sheet are usually not shown at their current market value*

An exception to this rule is when a mark-to-market exercise is done, for example for securities traded in the market regularly. In these cases, assets are revalued at their market price in the accounts. Usually, the notes to the accounts will have information on how value has been arrived at.

CASE STUDY: Robin's office

Robin, a business owner, found that after twenty-five years of running her business, its profitability was only marginally higher than it had been at the beginning whereas the property they had purchased twenty years before to serve as office space for the business was now worth more than ten times what it had been. With profits expected to be £250,000 prior to paying any rent, and the value of the property increasing to £4 million, a prudent decision would be to rent the property out and take a hit in business profitability by moving to a much smaller, rented office. Robin was able to rent the property for £200,000 and move the business to an office paying £50,000 in rent – a net gain of £150,000.

This decision would not have been obvious if we were just looking at the 'book' value of the asset.

Non-current assets

Non-current assets (sometimes called fixed assets) are assets which are of a longer-term nature and are not converted to cash frequently to meet the operational requirements of the business. They include tangible assets like machinery, buildings and land, plant and equipment, and intangible assets like goodwill. Other assets may be included (different businesses need different types of assets) and there may also be deferred long-term asset charges (for example, amounts paid in advance for benefits that accrue over more than 12 months).

Property, plant and equipment

The term 'property, plant and equipment' is used to encompass most long-term tangible and depreciable assets that the business owns.

Property the business owns, its manufacturing equipment and its vehicles are recorded in the Balance Sheet at their original cost, less accumulated depreciation. All equipment, machinery and buildings eventually wear out and need replacing. This wearing out is recognised on the P&L as depreciation. The Balance Sheet then records the accumulated depreciation over several years as a reduction in the value of the asset. The accumulated depreciation is the combined yearly allocation towards the cost of eventually replacing the depreciating asset. You may choose to reinvest this amount in the business to build capability to replace the asset when it wears out.

As an example, take the cutting machine we discussed in Chapter 4. It was bought for £1 million and was expected to last for ten years. The business accordingly depreciated the machine over its expected life by allocating £100,000 as an expense in each of the next ten years. By allowing this expense every year, the business recorded the value of the asset as decreasing over its expected ten-year life. In the second year, the asset will show on the Balance Sheet as a gross value of £1 million less depreciation of £100,000; in the third year, as £1 million less depreciation of £200,000 and so on, till it shows a net value of £0 at the end of the period. If the asset shows on the Balance Sheet as £600,000, this indicates that it is now four years old.

When looking at a business, a high value of accumulated depreciation relative to the value of the assets is an indication that the plant and equipment is quite old and may need replacing – incurring significant capital expenditure.

A business can choose to own its warehouse, office, manufacturing unit or to rent (or) lease these. It is important to recognise this as a separate decision when comparing the operating performance of different businesses in an industry. A business that does not own property may be nimbler but at the same time be vulnerable to rent increases.

> # *Key Principle: Renting or buying property is usually an investment decision – not an operating decision*

Assets such as strength of brand and customer base, team culture, employee loyalty, or relationships with suppliers and/or customers do not show on the Balance Sheet. Often, therefore, businesses that show a low value for non-current assets on the Balance Sheet may generate higher returns without a corresponding need to constantly reinvest in the business, potentially increasing the amounts of debt carried. Service-based businesses are an example of this: the investment required is usually a lot lower for sustainable profits to be generated.

Goodwill and intangible assets

Goodwill on business accounts specifically refers to any extra amount paid when purchasing another business, over and above the purchased business's net worth. In effect, what is commonly understood as goodwill – brand value, customer relationships, systems and processes built over several years, etc – only appear on business accounts when the business is sold and the buyer pays for them.

An increase in goodwill over several years usually indicates growth through acquisition.

> *# Key Principle: High and increasing goodwill usually indicates an acquisitive business*

Intangible assets are non-physical assets like patents, copyrights, trademarks, franchises or brand names. These usually show on the Balance Sheet when acquired from a third party – not when a business decides to value its own organic intangibles. Intangible assets with a finite life, like patents, are amortised over their expected life in the same way as tangible assets.

So, when value is attached to an intangible asset that has an expected life, this value is reduced every year. This reduction in value is called amortisation to indicate that it describes an intangible asset, not a tangible one. Amortisation, like depreciation, is accumulated on the Balance Sheet as a net value assigned to the intangible asset.

Given that a lot of the intangibles in businesses are never recorded on their balance sheets, often net worth is not a true indicator of the value of the business, though it is often used as a proxy for the value of a business on its last legs.

Other long-term assets

Long-term assets that do not strictly fall into the property, plant and equipment or goodwill and intangibles categories are reported in the Balance Sheet as 'other long-term assets'.

One such asset found quite often is long-term investments in shares, bonds, commodities and real estate. Investments in business subsidiaries and affiliates are examples of this. Long-term investments are usually reported at the lower of their cost price or market price, so the stated value may be misleading if they have gone up in value.

Another example of a long-term asset is prepaid expenses which refer to amounts that the business has paid for value that is to be delivered over multiple years.

Business owners might invest from within the business or take dividends and invest those in their personal capacity, and this choice is often driven by tax considerations. If a business has a lot of 'non-operating' investments, it is likely because it was tax efficient for the business owner to retain the profits within the business even though the business did not require the funds for its operations.

Current assets

Assets that are routinely converted to cash as part of the ongoing process of the business are referred to as current assets. For a business that sells products, cash is first used to buy inventory, inventory is then sold to customers on credit and becomes accounts receivable and finally, when the customer pays, accounts receivable convert back to cash. The business makes profit by consistently repeating this cycle. The different elements of the current asset cycle determine how efficiently the business can deploy its capital. 'Cash and cash equivalents', 'short-term investments', 'receivables', 'inventory' and everything that is either cash or can be converted to cash within a short period (usually a year) are current assets.

Cash and cash equivalents

A high amount of cash and cash equivalents (short-term investments) is usually an indication of a healthy business. Businesses may keep a substantial amount of cash to support operations, or because of the tax repercussions of withdrawing cash from the business. A consistently increasing quantity of cash in the business indicates good ongoing performance and generally a business with a lot of cash and low debt is stable and able to weather downturns in business. As the adage goes, 'turnover is vanity, profit is sanity, cash is a reality'.

Increasing piles of cash may also indicate that the business has found no potential avenues to deploy this cash to generate higher returns. As cash in the bank earns little interest, for most businesses it is better to employ the cash in business operations or in investments that produce an acceptable return. In this scenario, the management team needs to decide how much cash it needs in the business bank account and may think of any excess as employees with idle time, then ask themselves how they can make this cash work productively to improve the business.

> # *Key Principle: Money needs to work to make more money*

The inventory dilemma: Less or more?

Inventory, or stock, is the value of purchases and products that the business holds that have yet to be sold to its customers. A well running business will always know the exact value of its inventory (how much it has increased or decreased from the previous period) and conduct regular audits to confirm the value of inventory being recorded. As inventory is usually recorded at the lower of cost or market value, obsolete inventory should be systematically removed from the value recorded in the accounts.

Inventory usually varies in line with the sales of the business and a growing business often requires a growing inventory to ensure incoming orders are filled in good time. This implies that the ratio between inventory and cost of sales should remain similar. When this is not the case, it usually indicates either a poorly managed business or a business in an industry subject to economic vagaries.

The inventory turnover ratio seeks to determine and measure this relationship, and is defined as:

$$\text{Inventory turnover}$$
$$= \text{cost of goods sold} \div \text{average value of inventory}$$

This ratio indicates how quickly the business can convert its inventory to sales. As an example, if the average value of inventory in a year is £200,000 and the cost of goods sold is £800,000, the inventory turnover will be:

$$£800,000 \div £200,000 = 4x$$

which implies that the business turns over its inventory four times every year.

Another way to understand this number is to convert it to 'inventory days' by dividing the number of days in the period of measurement by the inventory turnover. In the above example, inventory days will be:

$$365 \text{ days} \div 4 = 91.25 \text{ days}$$

This implies that the business keeps 91.25 days' average sales in inventory at any point in time, to ensure that it continues to meet its current level of demand.

As inventory is an investment of capital, in most cases the lower this number, the better. If the business was able to keep only thirty days' inventory to meet the same level of demand, either through better inventory management or more efficient suppliers, it would have released a lot of capital that was previously stuck in the business. This is even more important for growing businesses as the constant need to increase investment in inventory may often constrain growth.

Accounts receivable: Being a bank

When a business sells its product or service and does not immediately receive cash payment, the outstanding amount is referred to as a receivable and the buyer is recorded as a trade debtor on the business's balance sheet. If, for example, business invoices are due thirty days after the invoice is issued, the invoice value is recorded as 'receivable' for thirty days, or until the buyer pays the invoice.

If some buyers do not pay their invoices, receivables may become 'bad debt' and be written off the books. The receivables figure in the accounts is therefore usually shown 'net', after adjusting for this bad debt.

A receivable days ratio indicates the number of days for which the business's receivables remain outstanding at any point in time. The ratio is defined as:

Receivable (or) debtor days = 365 days × average value of receivables ÷ net credit sales

As an example, if the average value of the receivables across the year is £258,000 and credit sales total £2,000,000, the receivable days will be:

365 days × £258,000 ÷ £2,000,000 = 47.1 days

This implies that the average customer pays the business 47 days after the invoice has been issued. Receivables can be considered as loans from the business to its customers – essentially the business acting as a bank by providing interest-free cash to its customers – and therefore, usually, the lower this number, the better. If the business was able to receive money within thirty days from invoice date, either through changing its credit terms or regularly following up with reminders to its customers, it would release a lot of capital to grow the business. Often businesses get caught in a receivables trap when they land large contracts that demand significantly higher levels of credit.

In the above example, if the business were to acquire a new customer willing to place a £500,000 order but only prepared to pay ninety days after invoicing, the receivable level and therefore the capital investment the new customer is asking for is:

$$£500,000 \times 90 \div 365 = £123,287.67$$

If the business does not budget for this additional capital requirement before accepting the order, it could be in danger of running out of cash – and potential bankruptcy. Unfortunately, sometimes the management team believes that growth solves all problems and commits to sales whenever it can – in some cases unwittingly pushing the business closer to bankruptcy in the process.

In competitive industries, a business may use longer credit terms to add value and differentiate their offer to potential customers. This could be a reasonable strategy for cash-generating businesses and businesses with easy access to capital. The receivable days ratio is therefore an important number to track in your strategy arsenal.

> # *Key Principle: Large customers who pay late could bankrupt your business*

In some countries (including the UK), P&L information for many businesses is not publicly available whereas balance sheet information is more readily available. If the accounts receivable information for a business is available and you have a reasonable understanding of the credit terms that are usually offered to customers in the industry, you can estimate the sales of the business.

For example, if the accounts receivable reported is £150,000 and the industry typically works on forty-five-to-sixty-day credit terms to customers, the business is likely to have sales between £900,000 and £1.2 million.

Other current assets

Non-cash assets that are not separately identified in the Balance Sheet and are due within the year are reported as 'other current assets'.

A key example is prepaid expenses, where the business has paid for goods and services but not received them yet. This could be anything from insurance premiums paid for the year to advance payments made to suppliers. Prepaid expenses sometimes indicate the bargaining power and credit rating of the business – a strong business would have low advance payments and would purchase most items on credit.

Another asset recorded here is deferred income tax, which arises when differences in tax reported in the financial and tax accounts lead to a difference between the payable income tax calculation and the actual tax expense.

8
Liabilities, Net Assets And Equity

Current liabilities

Current liabilities are the debts and obligations of the business due over the next twelve months. These could be operating liabilities – for example, payments due for purchase of inventory – or financial liabilities like bank debt.

For most businesses, liabilities are cheaper than equity as a source of funds and even within liabilities, operational current liabilities are often the cheapest source of funding. It is therefore important to view these as a source of capital and not just as an operating decision. The working capital cycle, which looks across the current asset cycle and the payables, determines how efficiently the business can deploy its short-term capital. This can be defined as:

Inventory days + receivable days
− payable days (see below)

Accounts payable: The right time to pay

When a business buys products or services and does not pay for these straight away in cash, the amount due is referred to as a 'payable' and the supplier is recorded as a trade creditor on the business's balance sheet.

If, for example, suppliers usually give the business thirty days to pay their invoices, the amount of purchase remains as a payable for thirty days, or until the business pays the invoice.

Like the receivable days, the payable days ratio indicates the number of days' average payables that the business has outstanding at any point in time. The ratio is defined as:

Payable (or creditor) days = 365 × average value
of payables ÷ cost of goods sold

As an example, if the average value of the payables across a year is £110,000 and the cost of goods sold is £800,000, the payable days will be:

365 days × £110,000 ÷ £800,000 = 50.2 days

This implies that, on average, the business pays its customers fifty days after it receives their invoices. Payables can be considered as interest-free loans taken from customers and therefore, usually, the higher this number, the better. If the business was able to pay ninety days from the date of the invoice, either through changing its supplier credit terms or changing suppliers, it would release a lot of capital to grow the business. Often management uncomfortable with debt and wanting to keep good supplier relationships pay bills as soon as they receive them, irrespective of the credit terms and often when their own invoices are outstanding for longer than their stated credit terms. This essentially amounts to refusing free credit in favour of unsecured debt – not a good strategy for most businesses.

In competitive industries, a business may use faster payments to suppliers as a competitive strategy to seek out the best suppliers. This could be a reasonable strategy for cash-generating businesses and businesses with easy access to capital. The payable days ratio is therefore another important number to track in your strategy arsenal.

Key Principle: Pay suppliers on time – not before time

Accrued expenses

Accrued expenses are liabilities that the business has incurred but has yet to be invoiced for. These expenses include taxes, wages and accrued rent payable in the future.

Most taxes due, including Value Added Tax and business tax payable when the final accounts are prepared every year, are included in accrued expenses.

Most people do not realise that paying employees in arrears is essentially asking them to fund the business for a week or a month – they deliver work for the entire period and build up the business's accrued expenses until they are paid their wages.

Other current liabilities

Liabilities that are not separately identified above and are due within the year are reported as 'other current liabilities'.

One of the most prominent is debt – the business's financial obligations that are due within the year. This is usually a combination of short-term debt, like business overdrafts, and the portion of long-term debt that is repayable in the short term. It is important to remember that the most common reason for business bankruptcy is neither poor performance nor decreasing sales – it's the business running out of cash. Having to pay back debt, especially large amounts of long-term debt, could lead the business to severe cash flow problems.

Other current liabilities include deposits received from customers and any payments received in advance from customers. As customer advances are usually included in the cash figure in current assets, it is important to remember that the cash amount in the business may not give us an accurate picture of its stability: some or a lot may just be advances received from customers, money being held on the customer's behalf until products and services are delivered. If they are not delivered (for whatever reason) that money may have to be repaid, which is why it is a current liability till such time as the product or service is delivered.

Non-current liabilities

Non-current liabilities are the debts and obligations of the business that are due more than twelve months in the future. These are usually either long-term financial debt or other long-term interests in the business.

Long-term debt

Long-term debt includes any debt with maturity more than a year away. Debt due within the year, including the part of long-term debt payable within a year, is called short-term debt and is part of the business's current liabilities.

Usually cash-rich and profitable businesses finance themselves even when they need to expand or make acquisitions. They seldom carry a large amount of long-term debt and usually their yearly net earnings are enough to pay off all long-term debt within a three- or four-year period, if not even faster.

At the same time, a business which has good earnings power and low debt potentially has a conservative management style and is not exploring all growth opportunities available to it. In these cases, management need to ask themselves the question – 'If funds for investment were not an issue, what opportunities could the business explore to grow and develop even faster?'

Often, the long-term debt in a business is directly linked to assets purchased by it. These may be property assets – offices and warehouses – or simply inventory that is funded by long-term debt.

In general, the rule for businesses is to keep the long-term debt low and focus on operational improvements and growth. This can change for one of two reasons – either when the asset requirement of the business is mostly long-term in nature or when the business is already performing well operationally and the capital invested in the business needs to be made to work harder for it.

 # *Key Principle: Use long-term debt for long-term investment requirements*

Deferred tax, minority interest and other long-term liabilities

All long-term liabilities that are not classified as long-term debt are categorised under this head in the balance sheet.

Deferred tax is tax that is due more than twelve months in the future. Minority interest is a figure representing the part of a subsidiary business that is not owned by the main business. This is often a result of consolidating accounts across businesses and is pretty much a balancing entry in the accounts and better analysed through the component it is there to balance, which will be found under the long-term investments.

Other long-term liabilities could include judgements against the business, benefits that it has promised to a person or entity that are payable more than a year in the future, interest on tax liabilities, unpaid fines and derivative instruments.

Net assets

The net assets of a business are the total assets, both current and non-current, less the total liabilities, both current and non-current. They are an indicator of the total investment in the business by the shareholders and are exactly equal to the total equity invested in the business.

While a net assets figure is usually given in the balance sheet, because it combines both operational and financial components it is often not a useful metric to analyse except to indicate the book value of what the shareholders have invested in the business and thus give a rough indication of the minimum amount shareholders could expect to receive in a sale of the business.

The net assets of a business are sometimes referred to as the net worth of the business. Changes in this number over time is one of the things credit agencies look at when rating a business.

Shareholders' equity: The book value of the business

The shareholders' equity (also referred to as the book value) of the business is the sum of the amount of money the business owners put in to start it and what they have left in the business, over time, to keep it operating. The net assets of the business equal the total shareholder's equity of the business – the two sides of the balance sheet balance.

The total equity or shareholders' equity is made up of share capital, which could have been raised in different ways, and retained earnings, which is the accumulated profit retained in the business over time.

Share capital

When starting a business, the business owner contributes an initial amount to fund the business. This might be expressed as so many shares, with a face value of so many pounds (or pence) each. Similarly, when new shareholders are brought into a business, new shares may be issued to them in return for their investment – this is referred to as an equity investment. The amount raised by the business through the sale of shares does not usually have to be paid back and belongs to the business to use; but terms and conditions may attach to it.

Broadly, shares could be common stock or preferred stock. Common shareholders are the owners of the business – they can appoint directors and share in its profits (through dividends), and they receive the proceeds when the business is sold.

Preferred shareholders are paid before common shareholders in the event of the business going bankrupt, and are also paid a dividend ahead of common shareholders (usually a fixed percentage of their investment). Apart from that, they usually do not have voting rights and have less say in the decisions of the business. Preferred equity has the nature of equity in that it does convey a stake in the business and the nature of debt in that the preferred dividend must be paid if the business has enough profits to afford it. But it does not have the tax benefit of debt as the payments on preferred equity are dividends which the business may not deduct from its tax bill. This makes it an expensive and unattractive source of funds for the business and its presence on the balance sheet usually indicates that in the past the business has struggled to source funds.

When shares are sold above their stated book value, the additional funds are recorded within share capital as 'paid in capital'.

Retained earnings: making money work

For most businesses, the retained earnings are a lot more indicative of the owner's stake in the business than the share capital.

This is because, for as long as the business has been in operation, the business owner has had a choice: it could either extract the profit after tax from the business or leave it in the business to help the business grow. When the profit is retained in the business, it is recorded as 'retained earnings'. Over time, therefore, the retained earnings are an amount the business owner has invested in the business.

Retained earnings is an accumulated number and every year, the retained earnings of a business increase by the amount of profit after tax not used to pay dividends or buy back shares. Similarly, if the business loses money or pays out more dividend than its profits, the retained earnings decrease.

As a valuable indicator of the net worth of the business, seeing a trend of increasing retained earnings is an important indicator of the strength and competitiveness of the business. While there are some exceptions to the rule, in general a growing and high retained earnings figure is indicative of a good business. This is because the more earnings a business retains, the faster it can grow and the further it can increase both earnings and retained earnings.

Key Principle: Retained earnings shows reinvestment in growth in the business

9
Reading A Balance Sheet

Liquidity analysis: Smart rules of thumb

One of the most important indicators of the health of a business is its operational liquidity. There are several ways of analysing the balance sheet to understand how likely the business is to face cash flow pressures and equally how competitively the business runs its operations.

Current ratio and quick ratio

Given the importance of short-term liquidity in ensuring a business survives, the current ratio, which compares the current assets to current liabilities, is an important metric to keep an eye on.

Current ratio = current assets ÷ current liabilities

As an example, if the current assets are £469,500 and the current liabilities are £134,000, the current ratio will be:

$$£469,500 ÷ £134,000 = 3.5x$$

The current ratio is an indicator of the liquidity of the business and answers the question 'if all short-term liabilities of the business had to be settled urgently, would the business be able to do this from its short-term assets?' The higher the ratio, the more liquid the business. A current ratio above one is considered good. If the current ratio is below one, the business may have difficulty meeting its short-term obligations to its creditors. Most financial institutions will look closely at a business's current ratio when deciding whether to lend to it and often require a covenant that the current ratio will stay above a certain level.

However, a lot of good businesses aim to keep their current ratio below one because they realise that their competitive position allows them to source cheap short-term debt and supplier finance, take advance payments from customers, keep low inventory levels and continue to keep their cash balances deployed – all of which lead to a low current ratio.

The quick ratio is often used by lenders to work out how easily they could recover their loans if they had to. The quick ratio is a stricter version of the current ratio and removes inventory and prepaid expenses from the numerator on the assumption that these are more difficult to convert to cash to pay off liabilities, especially if the business starts to struggle economically:

$$\text{Quick ratio} = (\text{current assets} - \text{inventory} - \text{prepaid expenses}) \div \text{current liabilities}$$

In the previous example, if the current assets include £200,000 of inventory and £10,000 of prepaid expenses, the quick ratio will be:

$$(£469,500 - £200,000 - £10,000) \div £134,000$$
$$= £259,500 \div £134,000 = 1.94x$$

A quick ratio above one indicates that the business has enough liquidity to meet any urgent requirements for operating cash.

Working capital

More businesses go bankrupt for lack of cash than for lack of profits. Often, when the economy is doing well businesses survive despite themselves – the margin of error is high enough to allow even businesses with bad processes to do well. However, the moment the tide turns and there is a shock to the economy, the need to work harder and smarter becomes critical, to survive and prosper. It is important therefore to remember to keep an eye on the cash level.

Working capital, also referred to as net current assets, is the difference between the current assets and current liabilities of a business and is another measure of its short-term financial health:

Working capital (net current assets)
= current assets − current liabilities

As an example, if the current assets are £469,500 and the current liabilities are £134,000, the working capital will be:

£469,500 − £134,000 = £335,500

A high, positive working capital indicates that the business can easily fund its current operations and invest in future activities and growth; but it may also indicate that management is being lazy and not investing excess cash properly. Equally, a negative working capital may indicate pressure on the business's cash flow but could also indicate competitive ability, i.e. that the business can influence its customers to pay in advance and influence its suppliers to extend favourable credit terms.

Cash gap: The cash conversion cycle

The cash gap is a useful way to measure why the business may be struggling with cash. Simply put, the cash gap refers to the number of days from when money leaves the business (through buying stock, paying suppliers, etc) to when money is received by the business from customers. The larger the cash gap, the greater the pressure on the cash flow.

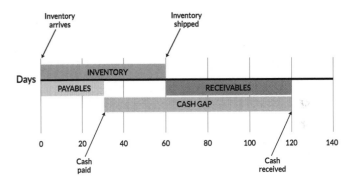

The cash gap – an easily visualised concept

This cash gap is also referred to as the cash conversion cycle:

Cash gap (cash conversion cycle)
= Receivable days + inventory days − payable days

As an example, if on average customers pay after 47 days, the business keeps 91 days of inventory and pays its suppliers 50 days after receiving bills, the cash gap will be:

= 47 days + 91 days − 50 days = 88 days

This indicates that the business needs operational funding worth 88 days of sales to continue to operate at any time. As a broad indicator, if the business is looking to add £1 million sales a year, it would need to budget capital of £241,000 (£1 million × 88 ÷ 365) to support this growth.

The business's cash gap is influenced heavily by the type of product or service it provides and the nature of its industry. Usually, consistent or decreasing cash gaps are positive as they indicate a stable or improving business.

A few easy strategies can help decrease your cash gap and release more money into the business.

For receivables:

- Reducing the length of credit offered to customers and, where possible, requiring up-front payments, incentivised through discounts

- Invoicing as soon as you deliver, or the right number of days before each agreed stage payment

- Sending regular reminders on unpaid invoices

For inventory and payables:

- Decreasing the amount of inventory held for each product

- Negotiating longer terms for paying suppliers

- Making payments at the end of the credit term, not before

The efficiency trap

For most businesses a cash gap analysis suggests that they need to reduce the gap by reducing receivables and inventory and increasing payables.

A handful of businesses, often ones that are strong in their marketplace, can push the cash gap into the negative – with payables being more than receivables and inventory together. This, in effect, translates to suppliers funding the growth of the business. When managed well, this can be a healthy position as the capital of the business is working efficiently.

But there is also an efficiency trap that you need to be wary of. This is where short-term funds begin to be used to fund long-term projects and assets and therefore are no longer available to shield the business if funds are urgently required. When banks have a 'run' and go under, it is often because of a spike in short-term withdrawals that cannot be supported because funds have been deployed by the bank in long-term or less liquid assets (assets that cannot be sold quickly and easily, should the need arise).

The same danger lurks in wait for businesses that begin to run such a tight, efficient ship operationally that they generate positive cash flow, and deploy it in long-term investments which are illiquid. This may happen in high-growth businesses where growth requires constant additional long-term investments. When, in this scenario, an urgent requirement for cash comes up, they cannot meet it and, caught in this efficiency trap, may see lenders and creditors take punitive actions, such as freezing business accounts, which could potentially bankrupt the business.

The key, therefore, is to measure and moderate working capital at all times to help the business grow sustainably.

 # Key Principle: Match short-term funds to short-term assets and long-term funds to long-term assets

Financial leverage analysis: Who's funding the business

Financial leverage indicates the composition of the money being used to fund the business. It can be measured by comparing debt, equity and assets.

A business with high leverage is likely to have a lot more ongoing cash flow pressure than a business with low financial leverage.

Debt to equity

The debt-to-equity ratio is a good indicator of what the business uses to finance its operations – debt or equity.

$$\text{Debt-to-equity ratio} = \text{debt} \div \text{shareholders' equity}$$

A business will have a range of different 'stakeholders' (parties with an interest in the business): the owner, other shareholders, the bank, debtors and creditors, its customers and, in some businesses, professional associations or regulators. Debt is usually defined differently by different stakeholders based on how conservative they are and what they are trying to achieve. Debt can be defined as total liabilities (current and non-current), long-term bank borrowings and various forms of external debt (long-term and short-term). The ratio is used to identify external financial leverage (rather than operating leverage); and external debt is therefore a good metric to use.

In the ratio, equity means total equity and includes retained earnings.

As an example, if the long-term debt is £2,629,000, there is no short-term debt and the total equity is £468,500, the debt-to-equity ratio will be:

$$£2,629,000 \div £468,500 = 5.6x$$

A good business usually maintains a debt-to-equity ratio below 0.8x. In cases where the key asset of the business is a property, funded by a commercial mortgage, a business may show high leverage even if the reason for owning the property was not strictly a business decision, rather driven by the owner's personal reasons. Irrespective, the business needs to be able to afford the debt and its ongoing payments and the debt-to-equity ratio is still relevant.

Assets to equity

The assets-to-equity ratio is another good indicator of whether the business finances its operations through debt or equity:

Assets-to-equity ratio
= total assets ÷ shareholders' equity

Assets can be defined as total assets or as non-current assets plus net current assets. The ratio indicates the proportion of assets that are financed by debt. As before, equity is total equity including retained earnings.

As an example, if the total assets are £3,251,000 and the total equity is £468,500, the assets-to-equity ratio will be:

£3,251,000 ÷ £468,500 = 6.94x

A ratio greater than two indicates that the business uses more debt than equity to finance its operations.

 # Key Principle: How your business is funded needs to be determined by a conscious strategy

10
The Cash Flow Statement

Why profits may not translate to cash

As most business accounts are drawn up using the accrual method of accounting (see Chapter 1), the Profit and Loss statement does not represent the actual cash movement in the business. Therefore, it is important for a business to separately measure and analyse cash movements (cash flow).

Most accountants do not create a cash flow statement, which sometimes leaves management puzzled when they see that they are making a lot of profit but never seem to have cash in the bank. Equally, the business may be performing poorly and only kept alive by constant infusions of funds from the business owner or other investors. Accordingly, it is imperative that the business has an internal set of management accounts that allows its managers to look at the cash flow in the business. The following table shows what a typical cash flow statement looks like; you may want to bookmark this page as reference. We systematically describe elements of this table in the rest of this chapter.

Net Income	£197,000
+ Depreciation and amortisation	£50,000
Changes in current assets	
Inventory	£5,000
Receivables	£158,000
Other current assets	£0
+ Changes in current liabilities	
Payables	£10,000
Accrued expenses	£1,000
Other current liabilities	– £10,000
+ Changes in other long-term liabilities	£20,000
Cash flow from operations	**£105,000**
– Capital expenditure	£130,000
+ Asset dispositions	£0
Cash flow from investing	**– £130,000**
Change in long-term debt	£46,000
Change in equity/ dividend paid	– £50,000
Cash flow from financing	**– £4,000**
Total cash flow	**– £29,000**
Beginning cash position	£30,500
Change in cash position	– £29,000
Ending cash position	**£1,500**

The cash flow statement indicates whether the business is bringing in more cash than it is spending (positive cash flow) or spending more cash than it is bringing in (negative cash flow). Like P&L statements, cash flow statements look at performance and movement of cash over a period of time by comparing the balance sheets at the beginning and end of the chosen period and noting how different components have changed.

The cash flow statement analyses these changes using different headings – cash from operations, cash from investments and cash from financing. These different streams of cash together equal the total cash flow, which is also the difference between the cash balances of the business at the end and beginning of the period being analysed.

Cash flow from operations

Cash flow from operations is the cash generated in the period from what your business actually does (as distinct from the decisions you take about financing). It adds depreciation and amortisation back to profit after tax as these are not movements of cash. It then accounts for cash that is released or deployed over the period in the operating areas recorded in the balance sheet.

A decrease in an operating asset means that cash tied up in the asset has been released into the business and this is recorded as an increase in cash flow and increases the cash balance available at the end of the period. A decrease in operating liabilities means that cash has been used to pay off some of those liabilities and this is recorded as negative cash flow and decreases the cash balance available at the end of the period.

An increase in current assets implies that cash has been used. This may be because of additional inventory being purchased, more credit sales or other increases in assets. Effectively, instead of receiving cash, the business has ended the period with more current assets. An increase in current assets is therefore a decrease in cash flow from operations and similarly a decrease in current assets is an increase in cash flow from operations.

An increase in current liabilities implies that cash has been released. This may be because suppliers have not been paid yet, or because more expenses or other current liabilities have accrued. Effectively, instead of using cash, the business has taken on more current liabilities over the period. An increase in current liabilities is therefore an increase in cash flow from operations and similarly a decrease in current liabilities is a decrease in cash flow from operations.

Like current liabilities, increases in other long-term liabilities also increase the cash flow from operations.

Cash flow from operations is the most accurate indication of the cash performance of the 'business part of the business' over the period, and it is often used by lenders to understand whether the business continues to be able to pay back debt.

In a good business, over time cash flow from operations tracks profit after tax. When these two numbers move in opposite directions or are not in sync, it usually indicates that the business's operations are not stable.

Profit is not cash

There are three fundamental reasons why profit and cash are different.

First, revenue is booked when sales are made and not when cash is exchanged. Thus, where cash is advanced by the customer to the business towards products or services that have not yet been delivered, cash increases whereas profits do not change. Equally, where goods or services have been delivered but the customer has not yet paid for them, revenue has been booked so profits have changed, but cash would not show an equivalent increase.

Second, expenses are matched to revenue and not to cash. You record the costs of goods or services when they are sold. Thus, when inventory is bought, it is not recorded as an expense and therefore does not affect profit. But cash has been used to buy that inventory, so the business's cash level decreases. Equally, when expenses are incurred on credit, profit decreases but cash does not (until those bills are paid).

Finally, capital expenditures are recorded as expenses over several periods based on depreciation schedules, which are often different from cash payment schedules for the asset purchased. As an example, where a business has bought a cutting machine for £1 million and decided to depreciate the cost over ten years (see Chapter 4), unless the payment for the machine is also scheduled over ten years, the cash payment schedule will be different from the depreciation schedule. In most cases cash is usually paid out sooner than the corresponding effect on profits.

How decisions affect cash

Given how important cash is for the survival of any business, the cash flow statement helps by breaking down the actions every decision-maker needs to take to influence cash in the business.

Selling to customers who do not pay early increases accounts receivable and reduces cash. Hoarding stock on incorrect predictions of what is likely to sell reduces cash. Deferring expenses increases current cash and inability to negotiate credit terms with suppliers reduces cash.

Savvy management would ensure that cash flow from operations is maximised by focusing on each individual component, to allow for cash to be invested without having to rely on cash flow from other sources of financing.

 # Key Principle: Cash flow from operations and
 profit after tax should track each other

Cash flow from investments

For businesses that rely on consistently investing to grow, the cash flow from investments is an important metric to understand. It comprises all use of cash in capital expenditure and all release of cash through asset dispositions.

Capital expenditures (sometimes shortened to capex) are outlays of cash or equivalents on non-current assets such as property, plant and equipment. They also include expenditures for such intangibles as patents. They are usually expensed over a period through depreciation or amortisation and therefore the full expenditure does not appear in the Profit and Loss of any one year.

For example, when a machine is bought for production, the expense is a capital expenditure and the value of the machine would be expensed through depreciation over its useful life. If a business needs to consistently invest in capital expenditure to stay competitive, the profit (or loss) by itself may not reflect the true comparative performance of the business and it would be important to look at the ongoing cash flow from investing. Usually, good businesses have low capital expenditures on an ongoing basis.

The cash flow to capex ratio is used to measure whether the business can cover its capital expenditure requirements with cash from operations or requires external financing support. A ratio of more than one indicates a stable business whereas a low ratio may indicate that the business needs to continue to invest to grow.

$$\text{Cash flow to capex}$$
$$= \text{cash flow from operations} \div \text{capital expenditure}$$

As an example, if the cash flow from operations is £105,000 and the capital expenditure is £130,000 this ratio will be:

$$£105,000 \div £130,000 = 0.81x$$

Another metric, easier to calculate, is the capex to earnings %, defined as:

$$\text{Capital expenditure} \div \text{profit after tax}$$

As an example, if the profit after tax is £197,000 and the capital expenditure is £130,000 this will be:

$$£130,000 \div £197,000 = 66\%$$

Strong businesses usually average a ratio below 50% over time.

> # *Key Principle: Investment and growth are correlated in sustainable businesses*

Cash flow from financing

Cash flow from financing is the cash generated from or used in financing activities. Since the main sources of financing are debt and equity, any changes in the values of debt and equity generate cash flow to or from financing.

If the business increases its debt, cash flows into the business whereas if the business pays back debt, the cash available in the business decreases.

Paying dividends and buying back shares usually require cash outflow whereas issuing new shares usually leads to cash inflow to the business.

While the cash flow from operations and the cash flow from investments are operational decisions, the cash flow from financing is a financial decision. It indicates the approach the finance department of the business has been taking to support the operations of the business. It is therefore useful to review the financial performance and the operating performance of the business separately by identifying how cash from financing flows over time.

Key Principle: How the business is funded is a decision – make sure it is one you have thought through

Mapping the financial statements

A useful way to understand the cash flow statement is to look at it as a derivative of the P&L statement and the balance sheets at the beginning and end of the period being analysed.

This can be detailed out as follows:

Cash flow statement		Profit & Loss Statement		Changes in Balance Sheet
Cash flow from operations	=	Profit after tax		
	+	Depreciation		
	+	Amortisation		
			−	Changes in current assets
			+	Changes in current liabilities
			+	Changes in long-term liabilities
Cash flow from investing	=			
		Changes in non-current assets		
Cash flow from financing	=			
		Changes in long-term debt	+	
	+	Changes in equity	+	

Change in cash balances	= Cash flow from operations
	+ Cash flow from investing
	+ Cash flow from financing

Effectively, the cash flow statement seeks to understand how much cash should have been generated in the period and where and in which form on the balance sheet that cash shows.

> # Key Principle: The Cash Flow statement is
> derived from the P&L and Balance Sheets

Cash flow projections

The cash flow statement, while a useful tool for analysis, only looks at past performance. Given the significant importance of cash in every business, it is important to also project how it will use cash and where it will source this cash.

For most businesses, a weekly projection of cash flow for the next three months is a good indicator that would highlight any crunch points that the business is likely to face.

This can be done quite simply by listing, week by week, all the cash expected to come in and go out over the next three months. Cash income is usually received from sales and receivables and can be analysed customer by customer or department by department. Cash outgoings include all expenses – salaries, purchases, tax payments and ongoing expenses.[6] While the business may generally be profitable and cash-positive, it may have particular periods in which it struggles for cash – salary payment weeks or tax payment weeks for example. Continually monitoring the next three months on a week-by-week basis prepares management for any issues that they may have to face and can proactively work towards resolving these.

Cash flow projections also give management specific goals to target through the projected period and, more importantly, questions to ask:

- Do supplier payments need to be delayed?

- Do we need to chase unpaid receivables before a certain date?

- Do we need to hold off on ordering stock until after salaries are paid?

- Do we have enough in the account for tax payments, or do we need to ask for deferral?

- When could the business need an overdraft and when do we need to start talking to the bank about it?

- When is the right time to buy extra machinery and vehicles?

---

6   If you would like a free template for projecting weekly cash flow, contact growthidea.co.uk.

CASE STUDY: Charlotte's payroll

Charlotte was used to dipping into her business overdraft every month to meet payroll. She had done this for years and knew that when customers paid, the business would always be back to having surplus cash. The constant need for overdraft however meant that she had to be really careful when she took on a new client as she would usually need to take on a fresh loan.

She felt that she always had the pulse of her business and had never used cash flow projections before. When she first looked at the cash flow projections drawn out by her finance manager, she was surprised that they did not indicate any requirement for bank finance. During payroll that month, when the business dipped into its overdraft again, she realised that her finance team was giving her monthly projections and what the business needed was week by week projections.

The week by week cash flow projections immediately highlighted something she had already known. Her payroll usually happened on the twenty-fifth of every month and her largest clients always paid towards the end of the month – usually on the last day of the month. Her cash flow issue and her reliance on the bank was down to just one week of mismatch between cash coming into the business and cash leaving the business.

She decided to make a drastic change in her business. She spoke to her entire team and they decided to move their payroll date to the first day of the following month.

With this one change, she was able to completely eliminate her reliance on the bank. The week by week projection allowed her to really drill down into the timing of any potential issues that the business may have with cash flow and take targeted decisions to solve these.

Unlike the statements, the projections look forwards. Most management teams are uncomfortable making less-than-conservative assumptions about cash that might be required and how much is likely to be available. Nevertheless, there is nothing to stop you from preparing both conservative and less conservative projections (other than time available, of course). It is important to build a forward view of the business, perhaps on a conservative basis if that is what the team is comfortable with, to ensure that the business does not run out of cash (or start to assume that this could never happen).

PART TWO
WINNING AT THE GAME OF BUSINESS – A WORKING CASE STUDY

11
Overview

Most business owners and managing directors start off as technicians in their business and do not have a background in accounting. This leads them to believe that the numbers of the business are best left to bookkeepers and accountants because they are the ones who have been trained to create accounts and would be much better at it. Often, they only look at their accounts once a year because the government has asked them to submit accounts annually and they also need to look at their tax calculations. What they inadvertently do in the process is ignore a goldmine of information that could help them lead their business to even greater heights while keeping it safe from the pitfalls that any business might run across.

This part of the book has been structured to teach the basics of practical accounting so you can create a set of accounts from scratch for a simple business. While it is not necessary to know how to keep your own financial accounts to be able to understand them, the understanding that comes from having worked on the building blocks of accounts and the confidence this gives you in becoming a professional businessperson are invaluable. This part takes you through a simple, fundamental way of keeping financial accounts, without having to get an accounting degree.

Once you can create business accounts from scratch, you will never be intimidated by business financials as you will have a practical understanding of the fundamental building blocks.

We will work together to build the accounts of a small business from start to finish and use in practice most of the numbers we have learned in Part One. The key message here is that it is simple to record numbers and understand your accounts and does not need to be complicated with jargon.

The four building blocks

Any transaction that brings money in or takes money out of the organisation can be classed as a financial transaction. Equally, sometimes you need to record transactions where no money has actually flowed – a financial transaction could just be money due to you or from you. A record of all such transactions becomes the financial accounts and it is little short of remarkable that every transaction can be summarised in one or both of two statements – the P&L and the Balance Sheet.

The P&L, as we have seen, boils down to

$$\text{sales} - \text{expenses} = \text{profit}.$$

The Balance Sheet is ultimately

$$\text{assets} - \text{liabilities} = \text{equity}.$$

Profit and equity are derived from just four types of transaction – sales, expenses, assets and liabilities.

Take a moment to reflect on that. Everything that happens in a business eventually finds its way beneath one of these four headings and there are only four possibilities for any transaction in the business.

To understand accounts from a 'non-finance' perspective, therefore, all we need to do is to look at every transaction that takes place in the business and assign it to either sales, expenses, assets or liabilities – and we will have our P&L and Balance Sheet ready.

The two choices every transaction comes down to

The method of accounting used across most of the world is the double-entry bookkeeping system. This, in simple terms, means that for every entry into one account, a corresponding and opposite entry is made in another account. As an example, if you buy a product for cash, the system records one entry as cash leaving the business and another as the product coming into it.

The words 'debit' and 'credit', which can sometimes acquire all kinds of obscure interpretations, are simply the terms used to denote the two parts of the double entry. One account needs to be debited and another needs to be credited. Debits record all money flowing out of an account while credits record all money flowing into it.

We've just seen that only four items make up the financial statements – sales, expenses, assets and liabilities. Among these, sales and liabilities are similar in that they both involve money coming into a business whereas expenses and assets involve money going out of it. Sales require money to flow into the account and liabilities almost always involve this, so both are recorded as credits. Expenses require money to flow out of the account and, sooner or later, you will have to pay for assets you acquire, so both are recorded as debits.

Let's take another moment to reflect on that. In essence, all financial transactions can be classified as bringing money in or taking money out – that's just two choices – not four!

   # Key Principle: All financial transactions simplify
   to 'money in' or 'money out'

The consumption test

To identify whether a transaction needs to be recorded as an expense or as an asset, we need to go back to the fundamentals of the financial statements. Remember that expenses appear on the P&L, which is a record of transactions over a period of time, whereas assets appear on the Balance Sheet, which is a snapshot – usually at the end of the P&L period.

This brings us to the concept of 'consumption'. Money that has been consumed before the date of the Balance Sheet is recorded as an expense. Money that has not been consumed before that date (e.g. money that is still in the business) is recorded as an asset.

A crucial example of this concept is the way raw material or inventory is recorded in the accounts. Only the amount of inventory that has actually been sold during the period covered by the P&L is recorded as an expense. The inventory still in stock as of the date on the Balance Sheet is an asset for the business.

We saw in Chapter 3 that accountants may rely on the business to report the value of inventory, which can lead to mis-estimating profitability for most of the year.

Instead of calculating gross profit as

$$\text{sales} - \text{cost of goods sold, with cost of goods sold}$$
$$= \text{beginning inventory} + \text{purchases}$$
$$- \text{ending inventory,}$$

they incorrectly estimate gross profit as

sales – purchases.

When inventory levels do not change dramatically, this can still give a fair approximation of performance. Unfortunately, it completely fails exactly when it begins to matter – when inventory levels start to vary dramatically. The consumption test is therefore crucial, to give an accurate picture of the performance of the business.

> # *Key Principle: It's only an expense if it has been consumed in the period*

12

Case Study: Riding Business Cycles With A 12-year-old

Armed with the fundamental principles, in the next five chapters, you will now embark upon building your own financial statements. We have been training business owners and management teams for over a decade based on the case study we now work through.[7] It presents accounting and management concepts in the simple world of a micro-business and covers the majority of what most business owners need to understand in their financial statements.

We will work alongside Koby, a 12-year-old, with a simple business – a lemonade stand – as he starts the business, manages it through a cycle of good and bad performance, and closes it down. As we work with

---

7   Contact growthidea.co.uk if you or your team would like to attend a workshop.

him, we will build a Balance Sheet, P&L and cash flow statements for the business, recording everything that happens in it.

Remember, business performance is captured in these three statements through debits and credits and through sales, expenses, assets and liabilities. And however complicated the business, the fundamentals remain the same.

Making the most of the case study

The case study walks through five operating periods in a business and we record transactions as they happen and as decisions are made. We show you how to build and change the financial statements as we go along.

To make the most of the case study, work alongside each decision. Whether you find it better to work with a pencil and eraser in this book, or separately, you will get the most out of this if you follow each decision Koby takes, map it on the financial statements and think about what the implications of different decisions might have been.

Each operating period should not take more than 30 to 40 minutes to actively work through and complete so, in three hours of work (or so) you will learn a bit more than what an MBA class often devotes a whole semester course to covering.

Starting the business

Koby, a 12-year-old, discovers his entrepreneurial streak. As a frequent visitor to the local farmers' market, he sees that visitors in the summer would probably welcome the chance to buy a refreshing drink.

He pulls together some initial research on the economics of a lemonade stand. He would need lemons, ice, paper cups and sugar. He knows that lemons cost 30p each and estimates that, if he bought in bulk, one cup of lemonade would need 10p worth of paper cup, ice, sugar and one lemon. He also estimates that he could easily sell each lemonade for £1 a cup.

Does that sound like a good business?

An effective way to answer this question would be to look at the gross margin of the business for each cup sold:

$$\text{Gross profit margin \%} = \text{gross profit} \div \text{turnover}$$
$$= (\pounds 1 - 30p - 10p) \div \pounds 1 = 60p \div \pounds 1 = 60\%$$

At a gross margin of 60% Koby has a potentially profitable enterprise ahead of him and decides to take the plunge.

Being new to business, he also decides to systematically record and measure everything that he does. He's heard his parents talking about Balance Sheets and decides to start there. He creates a simple table:

Things and stuff (assets)	What I owe (liabilities)
	What I own (equity)
Total	Total

You can see that this is the essential information for a Balance Sheet, with the assets on the left-hand side and the liabilities and equity on the right-hand side, so that assets = liabilities + equity.

Koby needs to put in his seed investment, so he invests his life savings of £5 in the business. He records this in his Balance Sheet:

Things and stuff (assets)		What I owe (liabilities)	
Cash	£5		
		What I own (equity)	
		Original investment	£5
Total	£5	Total	£5

He records this as cash on one side of the Balance Sheet and investment (equity) on the other side. Using this double-entry bookkeeping system, he has ensured that his Balance Sheet balances.

This is important to remember. Every time a transaction happens, it has two effects on the Balance Sheet – either equal on both sides or balancing on the same side (i.e. where a positive and a negative entry cancel out – we will see this later).

Koby knows that £5 will not buy enough ingredients – he does need to buy some material in bulk. What should he do to get more money to kick-start his business? He could take on a paper round, or a job, to raise funds; but he's conscious that the opportunity that he has spotted may be filled by someone else if he does not act immediately.

He therefore approaches a venture capital investor (his dad) and pitches his idea. The investor sees the merits of Koby's arguments and agrees to lend him £15 – on the condition that his books need to be transparent and correct. The investor offers a simple interest structure – £2 every week on the £15 loan.

Is that a good interest rate? Let's find out. The interest rate for a week is:

$$\text{Interest} \div \text{Principal} = \pounds2 \div \pounds15 = 13.33\%$$

This looks high, but palatable. But that's not the interest rate we usually think about and benchmark in our minds – we usually think of annual interest rates. Converting the above to an annual interest, i.e. over 52 weeks,

$$(1 + 13.33\%)^{\wedge}(52 - 1) = 669.81\%!$$

Now there's a shark investor if we've ever seen one. On the flip side, the real money in a successful business is in the equity gains for the business owner; and this investor has not asked for any equity. They are also investing in an untested entrepreneur with no business plan and no security to offer.

Koby decides he is going to make it happen and shakes on the deal. He immediately updates his books:

Things and stuff (assets)		What I owe (liabilities)	
Cash	£20	Loans	£15
		What I own (equity)	
		Original investment	£5
Total	£20	Total	£20

Again, note that the double-entry system means that the left side of the Balance Sheet increases by £15 (the cash loaned) and, at the same time, the right side of the Balance Sheet now records the loan amount.

Koby's market research leads him to estimate that he can sell between forty-five and sixty cups every weekend. For the first weekend, he decides to stock enough to provide fifty cups, and he buys for cash:

50 lemons for 30p each	£15
A 1 kg pack of ice (200 cubes) for 50p	£0.50
A ½ kg pack of sugar (100 spoons) for 50p	£0.50
50 paper cups for £4	£4
Total	£20

This will affect his cash balance (he's had to spend all he's got) but now he has a corresponding value in inventory. His Balance Sheet now looks like this:

Assets		Liabilities	
Cash	£0	Loans	£15
Inventory	£20	Equity	
		Original investment	£5
Total	£20	Total	£20

Koby has traded one asset (cash) for another (inventory). This is an example of two entries on the same side of the Balance Sheet cancelling out. Cash has decreased by £20 and inventory has increased by £20, ensuring that the total assets remain at £20 and the Balance Sheet still balances.

Koby is now ready for the weekend.

Koby's first day at the market

Koby arrives early, finds another trader who is willing to rent a bit of his stand for just £12 for the day and sets up. He knows he has a 60% gross profit margin. He will need to sell twenty lemonades to make a gross profit of £12 and be able to cover the rent.

This would be enough to break even if rent was his only administrative (or) overhead expense. In this simple scenario, rent is the fixed cost and the contribution margin is 60%.

Break-even sales = fixed costs ÷ contribution margin
= fixed costs ÷ [(sales − variable costs) ÷ sales]

$$= £12 ÷ ([£1 − 40p] ÷ £1) = £12 ÷ 60\% = £20$$
(i.e. twenty cups at £1 a cup)

With his stand set up, Koby now needs to take some important operating decisions. How much material should he use for his lemonade?

Too much lemon, ice or sugar may make the drink expensive to produce, or too sour, or too sweet. Similarly, too little lemon, ice or sugar would increase his profit margin but will probably make his drink unappetising and damage the new trader's reputation.

For each lemonade, he decides to stick to his original numbers and use four ice cubes and two spoons of sugar. Given what he spent to buy the ingredients (see table above), he works out the cost of each lemonade to be:

Lemon		£0.30
Ice	4 cubes × 50p ÷ 200 =	£0.01
Sugar	2 spoons × 50p ÷ 100 =	£0.01
Cups	1 cup × 8p	£0.08
Total cost of lemonade		£0.40

Koby prepares his first batch of lemonade, just as people begin to arrive at the market.

It turns out to be a hot day and he was right, there is a lot of demand for his refreshing lemonades. He has a successful day and sells forty cups at £1 each. As he closes his stall at the end of the day, he decides to take the time to also close his books. He creates his first P&L statement:

Sales (40 lemonades at £1 each)	£40
Cost of sales (40 lemonades at 40p each)	£16
Gross profit	**£24**

Koby has had a good day and decides to reinvest everything in his business. He updates his Balance Sheet to show £40 cash takings, £16 of inventory sold and the difference between the two items (the profit) recorded as retained earnings. The Balance Sheet continues to balance:

Assets		Liabilities	
Cash	£40	Loans	£15
Inventory	£4	Equity	
		Original investment	£5
		Retained earnings	£24
Total	£44	Total	£44

There are of course other costs that Koby must pay.

He had hired a small fridge for the day and needs to pay 50p for this. He also got a lift to the market and needs to pay 50p for the fuel. Additionally, he needs to pay the rent on the stall (£12) and the £2 interest on the money he borrowed from his dad. All of this comes both out of cash and out of retained earnings. Koby updates both his P&L statement and his Balance Sheet:

Sales (40 lemonades at £1 each)		£40
Cost of sales (40 lemonades at 40p each)		£16
Gross profit		**£24**
Administrative expenses		£13
Stall rent		£12
Fuel		£0.50
Fridge hire		£0.50
Operating profit		**£11**
Interest		£2
Net profit		**£9**

Assets		Liabilities	
Cash	£25	Loans	£15
Inventory	£4	Equity	
		Original investment	£5
		Retained earnings	£9
Total	£29	Total	£29

Koby has made £9 on his first day of business – for an initial investment of £5. As he sees it, that's a weekly return of £9 ÷ £5 = 180%. That is a very healthy business indeed.

What does not show on the financial accounts is that Koby has also built a lot of credibility in the market and some strong business connections during the day. One of his new connections happens to be the local bank manager, who indicates to Koby that he could get a loan from a bank now that he has some history in business.

With £25 of cash in hand, and given how expensive his current loan is, Koby decides that he would rather repay the loan from his dad and apply for a cheaper loan from the bank. This affects his Balance Sheet as follows:

Assets		Liabilities	
Cash	£10	Loans	£0
Inventory	£4	Equity	
		Original investment	£5
		Retained earnings	£9
Total	£14	Total	£14

With his first weekend completed, Koby now has his final accounts.

Koby's first set of scorecards

Koby's first Profit and Loss statement, for the first day at the market, is ready.

Sales (40 lemonades at £1 each)	£40
Cost of sales (40 lemonades at 40p each)	£16
Gross profit	**£24**
Administrative expenses	£13
Operating profit	**£11**
Interest	£2
Net profit	**£9**

His balance sheet can be presented in the more familiar format from the previous chapters:

Assets	This week (£)	Last week (£)
Property, plant & equipment	0	0
Goodwill & intangibles	0	0
Other long-term assets	0	0
Total non-current assets	**0**	**0**
Cash and cash equivalents	10	0
Inventory	4	0
Receivables	0	0
Other current assets	0	0
Total current assets	**14**	**0**
Liabilities		
Payables	0	0
Accrued expenses	0	0
Other current liabilities	0	0
Total current liabilities	0	0
Net current assets (liabilities)	**0**	**0**
Long-term debt	0	0
Other long-term liabilities	0	0
Total non-current liabilities	**0**	**0**
Net assets	14	0
Equity		
Share capital	5	0
Retained earnings	9	0
Total equity	**14**	**0**

He can also build and look through his cash flow statement, to understand how cash has moved in his business.

Net profit	£9
+ Depreciation and amortisation	£0
– Changes in current assets	
Inventory	£4
Receivables	£0
Other current assets	£0
+ Changes in current liabilities	
Payables	£0
Accrued expenses	£0
Other current liabilities	£0
+ Changes in other long-term liabilities	£0
Cash flow from operations	£5
– Capital expenditure	£0
+ Asset dispositions	£0
Cash flow from investing	£0
Change in debt	£0
Change in equity/ dividend paid	£5
Cash flow from financing	£5
Total cash flow	**£10**
Beginning cash position	£0
Change in cash position	£10
Ending cash position	**£10**

13
Growing The Business

With a successful first weekend of operations under his belt, Koby grows in confidence and decides to commit further to his business the next weekend.

He starts the second weekend with the Balance Sheet he created the previous weekend. Remember, the Balance Sheet at the end of the previous period is also the Balance Sheet at the start of the new period.

Koby now has a track record of success and can look to his new connections (the local banker) for cheaper sources of funding. He applies for, and gets, a loan of £50 – interest-free for the first week – and updates his Balance Sheet:

Assets		Liabilities	
Cash	£60	Loans	£50
Inventory	£4	Equity	
		Original investment	£5
		Retained earnings	£9
Total	£64	Total	£64

There is now a slight mismatch between the financial accounts and reality. Can you spot it?

As per accounting conventions, Koby has recorded his inventory at historical cost (what he paid for the ingredients) – £4. Lemons that are a week old are not ideal for a high-quality lemonade – especially in the initial stages of Koby's new lemonade business. Their value is likely to be less than £4. Koby does not really want to throw away old inventory or sell it at a loss. He decides to 'capitalise' his recent good behaviour at home and pitches an at-cost sale to his mum. His offer of ten lemonades for £4 convinces her and he is able to sell his entire inventory, with the following effect on his Balance Sheet:

Assets		Liabilities	
Cash	£64	Loans	£50
Inventory	£0	Equity	
		Original investment	£5
		Retained earnings	£9
Total	£64	Total	£64

With his war chest of cash and soaring confidence, Koby decides to double his investment in stock; and stock for selling 100 cups of lemonade, which involves purchasing:

100 lemons for 30p each	£30
Two 1 kg packs of 200 ice cubes for 50p	£1
Two ½ kg packs of sugar for 50p	£1
100 paper cups	£8
Total	£40

He has enough cash to buy the entire amount outright, with some left behind for other expenses. However, he realises that the previous weekend he had made a profit of £9 but still only had a cash balance of £10 – only £5 over his initial investment. With this new-found understanding that 'cash is king', he negotiates with all his suppliers to allow him 50% credit on stock. He therefore has to only pay out £20 in cash and is able to get credit for the remaining £20, making his Balance Sheet look like:

Assets		Liabilities	
Cash	£44	Payables	£20
		Loans	£50
Inventory	£40	Equity	
		Original investment	£5
		Retained earnings	£9
Total	£84	Total	£84

The Balance Sheet appears to carry a lot of cash, but in this case, it is cash that has really just been borrowed from the bank!

What do people with a lot of cash in the business often do?

Koby decides to make a long-term investment in his business (and in himself). He buys a trolley for £20 – his first capital expenditure. Now he does not need anyone to ferry his stock to the market and he can save on fuel costs. Is this a good decision?

Last week, fuel cost him 50p. He has therefore spent £20 to save £50p every day he goes to the market. The net saving as a percentage is $50p \div £20 = 2.5\%$ or, on an annual basis (assuming 52 weeks), $(1 + 2.5\%)^{52} - 1 = 261.11\%$!

Koby has invested money for which he is currently not paying any interest at 261.11%. Financially, this is a savvy decision. But by doing so, he has tied cash up in an asset that he could have rented and has increased the operating risk in the business. He has also altered the nature of his business from a nimble one to an asset-heavy business. He does get to play with his trolley and show it off to his friends all week – a perk of being a business owner! The purchase has the following effect on his Balance Sheet:

Assets		Liabilities	
Equipment	£20	Payables	£20
Cash	£24	Loans	£50
Inventory	£40	Equity	
		Original investment	£5
		Retained earnings	£9
Total	£84	Total	£84

Koby is now ready for his second weekend.

Koby's second day at the market

Koby arrives early at the market and sets up again with the trader he rented from last week. It is another balmy day and now most people in the market know him. He has both new and returning customers, and his selling skills have improved. He also decides to offer credit to customers so he can grow faster.

He has a successful day and sells eighty lemonades at £1 each – sixty for cash and twenty for credit. Each lemonade still costs Koby 40p. At the end of the day, his P&L statement for the second week in business looks like this:

Sales		
80 lemonades at £1 each		£80
Sale of inventory		£4
		£84
Cost of sales		
80 lemonades at 40p each		£32
Inventory sold		£4
		£36
Gross profit		**£48**

Koby's Balance Sheet now changes to incorporate the cash and credit sales and the change in inventory. He has used £32 of his £40 inventory and now also has debtors (receivables) of £20:

Assets		Liabilities	
Equipment	£20	Payables	£20
Cash £84		Loans	£50
Receivables	£20	Equity	
Inventory	£8	Original investment	£5
		Retained earnings	£57
Total	£132	Total	£132

As before, Koby still has other costs to pay. His fridge hire is now £1 and he needs to pay stall rent of £12. He updates his P&L and Balance Sheet to show this:

Sales	£84
Cost of Sales (40 lemonades at 40p each)	£36
Gross profit	£48
Administrative expenses	£13
Stall Rent	£12
Fuel	£0
Fridge Hire	£1
Operating profit	£35

Assets		Liabilities	
Equipment	£20	Payables	£20
Cash	£71	Loans	£50
Receivables	£20	*Equity*	
Inventory	£8	Original investment	£5
		Retained earnings	£44
Total	£119	*Total*	£119

Koby now needs to account for his trolley. It needs to be treated as capital expenditure, because it will help the business over multiple periods of time. He decides that the trolley will last him for four weeks and therefore to spread its cost over this period. This gives him a depreciation cost of £5 (£20 ÷ 4) for each of those weeks, making his Balance Sheet look like:

Assets		Liabilities	
Equipment £20 – Depreciation £5 =		Payables	£20
		Loans	£50
Net equipment	£15		
Cash	£71	Equity	
Receivables	£20	Original investment	£5
Inventory	£8	Retained earnings	£39
Total	£114	Total	£114

Before he closes his book, Koby decides to check with his debtors, to make sure they all remember they owe him money. This is, of course, a conservative approach, in accounting terms – recognising losses as soon as they are quantifiable. Once he starts calling around, he realises that one customer, who bought five lemonades, was not local and is no longer contactable. He decides to write off the £5 as bad debt, with this impact on his statements:

Sales	£84
Cost of sales	£36
Gross profit	£48
Administrative expenses	£23
Stall Rent	£12
Fuel	£0
Fridge Hire	£1
Depreciation	£5
Bad debt	£5
Operating profit	£25

Assets		Liabilities	
Equipment £20 –		Payables	£20
Depreciation £5 =		Loans	£50
Net equipment	£15		
Cash	£71	Equity	
Receivables	£15	Original investment	£5
Inventory	£8	Retained earnings	£34
Total	£109	Total	£109

The business this weekend has grown significantly and has also closed with a healthy amount of cash on the books.

Koby is now ready to close his books and create formal accounts for the weekend.

Koby's second set of scorecards

Koby's second P&L statement is set out below.

Sales	£84
Cost of sales	£36
Gross profit	£48
Administrative expenses	£23
Operating profit	**£25**

His formal Balance Sheet can be updated as follows:

Assets	This week (£)	Last week (£)
Property, plant & equipment	15	0
Goodwill & intangibles	0	0
Other long-term assets	0	0
Total non-current assets	15	0
Cash and cash equivalents	71	10
Inventory	8	4
Receivables	15	0
Other current assets	0	0
Total current assets	94	14
Liabilities		
Payables	20	0
Accrued expenses	0	0
Other current liabilities	0	0
Total current liabilities	20	0
Net current assets (liabilities)	74	0
Long-term debt	50	0
Other long-term liabilities	0	0
Total non-current liabilities	50	0
Net assets	39	0
Equity		
Share capital	5	5
Retained earnings	34	9
Total equity	39	14

He can also update his cash flow statement:

Net profit	£25
+ Depreciation and amortisation	£5
– Changes in current assets	
Inventory	£4
Receivables	£15
Other current assets	£0
+ Changes in current liabilities	
Payables	£20
Accrued expenses	£0
Other current liabilities	£0
+ Changes in other long-term liabilities	£0
Cash flow from operations	**£31**
– Capital expenditure	£20
+ Asset dispositions	£0
Cash flow from investing	**–£20**
Change in debt	£50
Change in equity/ dividend paid	£0
Cash flow from financing	**£50**
Total cash flow	**£61**
Beginning cash position	£10
Change in cash position	£61
Ending cash position	**£71**

14
A Shock To The Business

With two successful weekends of operations and a lot of learning under his belt, Koby, now an experienced entrepreneur, approaches his third weekend at the market. He starts preparing for this weekend by looking at the balance sheet he drew up at the end of the second weekend.

Given the much higher inventory left over from the last weekend, Koby decides that his volume of business is high enough that he may as well continue to use the older lemons, mixing them with the newer ones, rather than sell them at cost. As he has enough stock to make twenty lemonades, he decides to buy enough stock to allow him to make eighty more.

There's some shocking news awaiting when he heads over to the shop to buy lemons. The price has doubled over the week, apparently because a ship got stuck in a canal somewhere. Given the supply squeeze, suppliers are also unwilling to extend credit this week.

While he is not quite sure whether his supplier is taking advantage of his success, he decides to commit to eighty lemonades and purchases:

80 lemons for 60p each	£48
A 1.6 kg pack of 320 ice cubes for 80p	£0.80
A 0.8 kg pack of sugar for 80p	£0.80
80 paper cups	£6.40
Total	£56

For each lemonade, he decides to stick to his original recipe and use four ice cubes and two spoons of sugar. The price of ice cubes, sugar and cups has not gone up, so he works out the cost of each lemonade as:

Lemon		£0.60
Ice	As before	£0.01
Sugar	As before	£0.01
Cups	As before	£0.08
Total cost of lemonade		£0.70

Given that Koby's sale price has not increased whereas the cost of lemons has shot up, his margins are under tremendous pressure:

Gross profit margin % = gross profit ÷ turnover
$$= (£1 - 70p) \div £1 = 30p \div £1 = 30\%$$

With a gross margin of only 30%, the economics of the business have significantly deteriorated and Koby now needs to sell a lot more just to keep his business profitable. The effect on his Balance Sheet is:

Assets		Liabilities	
Net equipment	£15	Payables	£20
Cash	£15	Loans	£50
Receivables	£15	Equity	
Inventory	£64	Original investment	£5
		Retained earnings	£34
Total	£109	Total	£109

Koby also decides that, given that he cannot always sell remaining stock to his mum, he needs to have his own refrigerated storage cabinet to keep his inventory safe. Another asset purchase – this time his Balance Sheet is not as healthy as he would like it to be, but he is of course about to make a lot of cash over the weekend.

He purchases a storage cabinet for £10. The cabinet was appraised at £8 but Koby wanted to make the owner an offer he could not refuse and is confident of making the cost back quickly. He has bought assets before and is clearly a successful business owner! He pays £5 up-front with a promise to pay the remainder after the weekend.

The £2 that Koby has paid over and above the appraised value of the storage cabinet is referred to in accounts as a 'goodwill' payment. He updates his Balance Sheet to show his newest acquisition. This affects a few entries – an increase in tangible assets (storage cabinet) of £8, an increase in intangible assets (goodwill) of £2, a decrease in cash of £5 and finally the balance of £5 is recorded as an increase in liabilities:

Assets		Liabilities	
Net equipment £15 + £8 = £23		Payables	£20
Goodwill	£2	Loans	£50
Cash	£10	Other liabilities	£5
Receivables	£15	Equity	
Inventory	£64	Original investment	£5
		Retained earnings	£34
Total	£114	Total	£114

Koby is now ready for the third weekend.

Koby's third day at the market

A disciplined professional, Koby again arrives early at the market and sets up with the trader from whom he has rented for the last two weekends. Burned by the bad debt he incurred last weekend, he has also made up his mind to no longer offer credit.

It's a grey and rainy day, unfortunately, and footfall is a lot lower, as are the people wanting a drink. Business does go through cycles and one of the things every business needs to prepare for is for the cycle to turn. Koby immediately realises that making such a large investment in inventory today, without checking the weather forecast, may not have been a good idea. A combination of the weather and the no-credit policy means that Koby can only sell forty lemonades at £1 each. More than half his stock remains unsold.

As he sits down at the end of the day to calculate his profit, he realises that his stock contained both lemons bought at 30p and lemons bought at 60p. They are now all mixed up and he does not remember which ones he actually used. He has a choice over what to report as sold; a lemonade made from a 30p lemon costs 40p whereas a lemonade made from a 60p lemon costs 70p. If Koby uses first in, first out (FIFO) to record inventory, his P&L statement would show:

Sales (40 lemonades at £1 each)	£40
Cost of sales	
20 lemonades at 40p each	£8
20 lemonades at 70p each	£14
Gross profit	**£18**

However, if Koby records inventory as last in, first out (LIFO), his P&L would show:

Sales (40 lemonades at £1 each)	£40
Cost of sales	
20 lemonades at 70p each	£28
Gross profit	**£12**

When inventory costs are going up, a business can use LIFO to increase costs, decrease profits and taxes, and store value in inventory. Often, if businesses don't need to regularly report numbers to investors or a Board, they buy more and more stock to try and build competitive advantage. This expense does decrease profit in the short run, but there is value being stored in the increased stock.

Koby decides that, given that lemons lose value over time, it makes more sense to use FIFO reporting – he just needs to make sure that, going forward, he does actually use the older lemons first. FIFO means that he reports a higher profit. He then updates his Balance Sheet:

Assets		Liabilities	
Net equipment	£23	Payables	£20
Goodwill	£2	Loans	£50
Cash	£50	Other liabilities	£5
Receivables	£15	Equity	
Inventory	£42	Original investment	£5
		Retained earnings	£52
Total	£132	Total	£132

As before, Koby still has other costs to pay including his stall rent of £12.

He is also getting uncomfortable with his increasing debt; he is due to pay off the £5 debt on the storage cabinet and he decides to also pay off £10 of the bank debt. He calculates that he must also pay the bank £1 in interest. He updates his Balance Sheet with these transactions:

Assets		Liabilities	
Net equipment	£23	Payables	£20
Goodwill	£2	Loans	£40
Cash	£22	Equity	
Receivables	£15	Original investment	£5
Inventory	£42	Retained earnings	£39
Total	£104	Total	£104

One of Koby's credit customers pays £10. Koby records this as an increase in cash and a decrease in receivables.

Koby now notices that someone has broken the handle of his storage cabinet. He spends £6 to repair the handle. At this point he could choose to capitalise this repair expense and spread it over the life of the storage cabinet, which would help him report a higher profit for the period, but given he has chosen FIFO and pushed up his profit a bit, he decides to conservatively treat the entire repair cost as an expense incurred and settled in this period. This means that his cash decreases by £6 and his retained earnings decrease by the same amount. Do you see how decisions you take are reflected in your business's accounts? Remember, these choices are what makes financial accounting an art!

Koby decides to buy a £4 lock to protect what is now a reasonable amount of inventory. He regards the lock as a long-term asset and so decides to treat it as not depreciating. He records the transaction as a decrease in cash and an increase in net equipment.

The updated P&L and Balance Sheet look like this:

Sales	£40
Cost of sales	
20 lemonades at 40p each	£8
20 lemonades at 70p each	£14
Gross profit	**£18**
Administrative expenses	£18
Stall rent	£12
Repairs	£6
Operating profit	**£0**
Interest	£1
Net loss	**£1**

Assets		Liabilities	
Equipment £23 + Lock £4 = Net equipment	£27	Payables	£20
		Loans	£40
Goodwill	£2		
Cash	£22	Equity	
Receivables	£5	Original investment £5	
Inventory	£42	Retained earnings £33	
Total	£98	Total	£98

Koby also finds that he needs to dispose £7 worth of lemonade (ten lemonades) that he had made in anticipation of sale and cannot really keep for another week. This is simply an expense – like a depleting asset that has to just be written off as a decrease in inventory and retained earnings.

He records depreciation of £5 on his trolley and decides to adopt the same policy on his storage cabinet, depreciating it over four weeks, so counts depreciation expense for the first week as £2 (£8 ÷ 4). Most international accounting standards do not allow you to treat goodwill as expenses, so it just remains on the Balance Sheet, which now looks like:

Things and stuff (assets)		What I owe (liabilities)	
Equipment £27		Payables	£20
– Depreciation £7		Loans	£40
= Net equipment	£20		
Goodwill	£2		
Cash	£22	What I own (equity)	
Receivables	£5	Original investment £5	
Inventory	£35	Retained earnings £19	
Total	£84	Total	£84

Koby also received his first customer complaint this week! A customer claimed that her lemonade tasted of stale lemons and made her feel quite queasy. He was able to use his charm to prevent the situation from escalating but the incident certainly made him think. Now that he is running a regular business, he decides he needs to have product liability insurance. He pays £6 cash for the insurance, to cover him for three weeks.

The insurance is treated like a depreciating asset: recorded as a £2 expense (£6 ÷ 3) and a £4 asset – a prepaid expense which will reduce over the next two weeks.

Koby's Balance Sheet now looks like this:

Assets		Liabilities	
Net equipment	£20	Payables	£20
Goodwill	£2	Loans	£40
Cash	£16	Equity	
Receivables	£5	Original investment	£5
Inventory	£35	Retained earnings	£17
Prepaid expenses	£4		
Total	£82	Total	£82

It has been a difficult weekend for Koby – his first loss-making period. It did seem as though everything that could have gone wrong did go wrong this weekend.

He is glad to finally close his accounts.

Koby's third set of scorecards

Sales	£40
Cost of sales	
20 lemonades at 40p each	£8
20 lemonades at 70p each	£14
Gross profit	**£18**
Administrative expenses	£34
Stall rent	£12
Repairs	£6
Insurance	£2
Wastage	£7
Depreciation	£7
Operating profit	**–£16**
Interest	£1
Net profit (loss)	**–£17**

SCORE

Assets	This week (£)	Last week (£)
Property, plant & equipment	20	15
Goodwill & intangibles	2	0
Other long-term assets	0	0
Total non-current assets	**22**	**16**
Cash and cash equivalents	16	71
Inventory	35	8
Receivables	5	15
Other current assets	4	0
Total current assets	**60**	**94**
Liabilities		
Payables	20	20
Accrued expenses	0	0
Other current liabilities	0	0
Total current liabilities	20	20
Net current assets (liabilities)	**40**	**74**
Long-term debt	40	50
Other long-term liabilities	0	0
Total non-current liabilities	**40**	**50**
Net assets	22	39
Equity		
Share capital	5	5
Retained earnings	17	34
Total equity	**22**	**39**

Net profit	−£17
+ Depreciation and amortisation	£7
− *Changes in current assets*	
Inventory	£27
Receivables	−£10
Other current assets	£4
+ *Changes in current liabilities*	
Payables	£0
Accrued expenses	£0
Other current liabilities	£0
+ Changes in other long-term liabilities	£0
Cash flow from operations	**£31**
− Capital expenditure	£14
+ Asset dispositions	£0
Cash flow from investing	−£14
Change in debt	−£10
Change in equity/ dividend paid	£0
Cash flow from financing	**−£10**
Total cash flow	**−£55**
Beginning cash position	£71
Change in cash position	−£55
Ending cash position	**£16**

15
Turning Business Performance Around

Veteran business owner Koby decides to change strategy in his fourth weekend of operation. He decides he will invest in product quality and business stability and look to recover ground lost the previous weekend, by turning his business around.

As before, he starts his fourth weekend with the balance sheet he created for the previous weekend (at the end of Chapter 14).

With a lot of stock left over from the previous week and only a little cash, Koby decides that he does not want to buy more stock this week and will focus on clearing the stock he already has. The travails of the previous week have sent him desperately looking for some business know-how and he's been reading business books. One book that really resonated suggested differentiating his product to make a better margin and attract loyal customers. He decides to reinvent his product as a 'mocktail'.

He purchases mint leaves, straws and paper umbrellas for £5 credit. He then hires his first employee, his sister, to help him create exciting mocktails. He promises to pay her £5 for the brilliant work she promises to do. He records this as an increase in his other liabilities and a reduction in his retained earnings.

His inventory consists of fifty lemons and related material for fifty lemonades and is recorded in his accounts at a cost of £35 (70p per lemonade). Spreading the £5 cost of the mocktail material over the fifty drinks, increases the cost of each drink to 80p and total inventory to £40.

With the additional investment, Koby has transformed his £1 lemonades to £1.50 mocktails. The mocktail strategy is a direct focus on increasing the gross margin of the business:

$$\text{Gross profit margin } \% = \text{gross profit} \div \text{turnover}$$
$$= (£1.50 - 60p - 10p - 10p) \div £1.50$$
$$= 70p \div £1.50 = 46.67\%$$

While margins are no longer as high as they were when Koby first started, they are now reasonably better than margins last weekend.

Koby revises his Balance Sheet before he heads out to the market:

Assets		Liabilities	
Net equipment	£20	Payables	£25
Goodwill	£2	Loans	£40
Cash	£16	Other liabilities	£5
Receivables	£5	*Equity*	
Inventory	£40	Original investment	£5
Prepaid expenses	£4	Retained earnings	£12
Total	£87	*Total*	£87

He is now ready for the weekend.

Koby's fourth day at the market

As always, Koby arrives early to set up his stall.

It's another grey day, but now Koby has a string of strategies he is ready to deploy. He has worked hard on his sales script, added value to his now-differentiated product and reintroduced a credit policy for local customers who he recognises as regular visitors. His persistence and charm work their magic, too.

He sells forty mocktails at £1.50 each, thirty for cash and ten on credit. Sales remain tough owing to the weather and the higher price but each sale now generates more profit for Koby than last weekend. His P&L statement and Balance Sheet now look like this:

Sales (40 mocktails at £1.50 each)	£60
Cost of sales (40 mocktails at 80p each)	£32
Gross profit	**£28**

Assets		Liabilities	
Net equipment	£20	Payables	£25
Goodwill	£2	Loans	£40
Cash	£61	Other liabilities	£5
Receivables	£20	*Equity*	
Inventory	£8	Original investment	£5
Prepaid expenses	£4	Retained earnings	£40
Total	£115	*Total*	£115

As before, Koby still has other costs to pay – stall rent of £12, bank interest of £1, depreciation of £5 for the trolley and £2 for the storage cabinet, employee wages of £5 and the insurance charge of £2 for the weekend.

It's important to remember that some of these are cash expenses and others are non-cash expenses. Neither depreciation nor the insurance charge affect his cash balance in this period because the cash outflow for these items happened in a previous period. He updates his records to show these transactions:

Sales (40 mocktails at £1.50 each)	£60
Cost of sales (40 mocktails at 80p each)	£32
Gross profit	**£28**
Administrative expenses	£26
Stall rent	£12
Insurance	£2
Depreciation	£7
Wages	£5
Operating profit	**£2**
Interest	£1
Net loss	**£1**

Assets			Liabilities	
Equipment £20			Payables	£25
– Depreciation £7			Loans	£40
= Net equipment		£13		
Goodwill		£2		
Cash	£61 – £18 = £43		Equity	
Receivables		£20	Original investment £5	
Inventory		£8	Retained earnings £18	
Prepaid expenses		£2		
Total		£88	Total	£88

The weekend has not been very profitable, but having sold the same number of drinks as the previous weekend for a small profit is a bit of a relief for Koby.

Some of his credit customers pay him £10 and he decides to pay off all his suppliers with the cash he now has available, and to pay a further £10 off the bank loan.

His Balance Sheet now looks like this:

Assets		Liabilities	
Net equipment	£13	Payables	£0
Goodwill	£2	Loans	£30
Cash	£18	Equity	
Receivables	£10	Original investment	£5
Inventory	£8	Retained earnings	£18
Prepaid expenses	£2		
Total	£53	Total	£53

Having successfully navigated another difficult weekend and turned his business around, Koby sits down to close his accounts again.

Koby's fourth set of scorecards

Koby's fourth P&L statement is set out below.

Sales (40 mocktails at £1.50 each)	£60
Cost of sales (40 mocktails at 80p each)	£32
Gross profit	**£28**
Administrative expenses	£26
Stall rent	£12
Insurance	£2
Depreciation	£7
Wages	£5
Operating profit	**£2**
Interest	£1
Net loss	**£1**

His formal Balance Sheet can be updated as follows:

Assets	This week (£)	Last week (£)
Property, plant & equipment	13	20
Goodwill & intangibles	2	2
Other long-term assets	0	0
Total non-current assets	15	22
Cash and cash equivalents	18	16
Inventory	8	35
Receivables	10	5
Other current assets	2	4
Total current assets	38	60
Liabilities		
Payables	0	20
Accrued expenses	0	0
Other current liabilities	0	0
Total current liabilities	0	20
Net current assets (liabilities)	38	40
Long-term debt	30	40
Other long-term liabilities	0	0
Total non-current liabilities	30	40
Net assets	23	22
Equity		
Share capital	5	5
Retained earnings	18	17
Total equity	23	22

His updated cash flow statement would be:

Net income	£1
+ Depreciation and amortisation	£7
− Changes in current assets	
Inventory	−£27
Receivables	£5
Other current assets	−£2
+ Changes in current liabilities	
Payables	−£20
Accrued expenses	£0
Other current liabilities	£0
+ Changes in other long-term liabilities	£0
Cash flow from operations	**£12**
− Capital expenditure	£0
+ Asset dispositions	£0
Cash flow from investing	£0
Change in debt	−£10
Change in equity/ dividend paid	£0
Cash flow from financing	**−£10**
Total cash flow	**£2**
Beginning cash position	£16
Change in cash position	£2
Ending cash position	**£18**

16
Closing And Analysing The Business

As Koby closes his books, his mum walks in with some exciting news. The whole family is going on a six-week vacation to Japan.

But this means that Koby will have to close his business. Over the next week, he starts the process of winding down his operations.

His balance sheet at the beginning of the week, after the fourth weekend, was:

Assets		Liabilities	
Net equipment	£13	Loans	£30
Goodwill	£2		
Cash	£18	*Equity*	
Receivables	£10	Original investment	£5
Inventory	£8	Retained earnings	£18
Prepaid expenses	£2		
Total	£53	*Total*	£53

He collects all his receivables, disposes of his inventory at cost price and manages to find a buyer for his trolley and storage cabinet, who is willing to pay him their depreciated value of £13. He also manages to get a refund on the unused insurance of £2.

Recording these transactions changes the Balance Sheet to:

Assets		Liabilities	
Net equipment	£0	Loans	£30
Goodwill	£2		
Cash	£51	*Equity*	
Receivables	£0	Original investment	£5
Inventory	£0	Retained earnings	£18
Prepaid expenses	£0		
Total	£53	*Total*	£53

He uses the cash received to pay back the loan. He learns that he also has to pay a £2 prepayment charge on the loan.

His P&L looks like this:

Sales (all assets)	£13
Cost of sales (depreciated value of assets)	£13
Gross profit	£0
Administrative expenses	£2
Prepayment charge	£2
Operating profit (loss)	–£2
Net profit (loss)	–£2

Koby's Balance Sheet after the sale of the assets and prepayment charge looks like this:

Assets		Liabilities	
Goodwill	£2	Loans	£0
Cash	£19	Equity	
		Original investment	£5
		Retained earnings	£16
Total	£21	Total	£21

He then issues himself a dividend of the remaining cash (£19) and records his closing transactions:

Assets		Liabilities	
Goodwill	£2	Loans £0	
Cash	£0	Equity	
		Original investment	£5
		Retained earnings	−£3
Total	£2	Total	£2

Note that the intangible goodwill remains on the accounts unless someone buys the business.

At the end of four weeks' trading, Koby has taken a total of £19 from the business – on an initial investment of £5. A lot of demanding work, but not an insignificant return on capital for four weeks of work.

Summarising business performance

Koby's business performance over the four-week period is tabulated below. Over the period, the business enjoyed one good week and faced one bad week. Overall, it was a profitable business and Koby got quite a good return on his initial investment.

	Week 1	Week 2	Week 3	Week 4	Average	Total
Sales	£40	£84	£40	£60	£56	£224
Cost of sales	£16	£36	£22	£32	£27	£106
Gross profit	£24	£48	£18	£28	£30	£118
Expenses	£15	£23	£35	£27	£25	£100
Profit	£9	£25	-£17	£1	£5	£18

A common-size analysis

A straightforward way of comparing performance metrics over time is the common-size statement.

This uses the sales figures for each period as the base to look at all the components of the P&L as a percentage of sales. It allows us to look beyond the value changes that occurred during the period and focus on the relative changes in costs that have driven the changes in profitability.

Koby's business figures are presented below.

	Week 1	Week 2	Week 3	Week 4	Average	Total
Sales	100%	100%	100%	100%	100%	100%
Cost of sales	40%	43%	55%	53%	47%	47%
Gross profit	60%	57%	45%	47%	53%	53%
Expenses	38%	27%	88%	45%	45%	45%
Profit	23%	30%	-43%	2%	8%	8%

The numbers show that while the business started at a healthy gross margin, the increase in the price of lemons had a severe effect in week three. Koby was able to change tack, improve strategy and started moving the margin up in week 4.

Creating the map

The financial statements we created in this part attempt to capture and reflect the reality of Koby's business. The map is not the territory and we can see that if we had taken different decisions on capitalisation, depreciation and valuing inventory, the numbers might have looked different.

As Koby worked through different periods, we recorded and created a map of his business and the changes it went through using financial statements. Every change in the fortunes of the business was reflected in the financial statements. Equally, looking at the financial statements gives us a significant amount of information about Koby's business – as it would about any business, whether dealing in lemonade or not.

As you have worked through the different periods, you have also recorded a significant majority of the typical transactions a business goes through over time. You have also looked at the importance of understanding these numbers to be able to constantly keep your finger on the pulse of the business and adapt strategy when required.

Koby flies off to Japan, keeping his eyes open for new opportunities. He understands that his first business was just a learning ground for many greater things to come!

PART THREE
THE NEXT LEVEL OF PERFORMANCE

A few financial concepts bring together the best ways of understanding the performance of a business by combining knowledge gleaned from various parts of the financial statements. This part focuses on these concepts. We seek to delve deeper into what a business really needs to be measuring and working towards improving at a higher, consolidated level of value creation. We then relate back to different parts of analyses that tie into this consolidated picture to understand where each individual component fits.

To build a set of key metrics that indicate how the business is performing, we need to understand the relative importance of various metrics and ratios. We explore this in Chapter 17 using the DuPont framework, which brings together operational and financial comparisons and is one of the most useful ways for a management team to understand where they need to focus on to improve performance. The framework also helps create a powerful scorecard for your business – pointing out performance and an understanding of what's driving that performance.

Management needs to ensure that their business is structured to maximise its value and key to this is understanding how businesses are valued. Chapter 19 looks at ways in which established businesses are valued and why some methods are more popular than others.

17
Measuring Returns And Value Creation

To measure the value the business creates, you need to first measure the return that capital deployed in the business is able to generate and compare this against what the capital costs – often in opportunity costs.

The principle here is that every business owner has a choice over how to deploy their money (capital). Among several options available to them, they can invest it in bank deposits, use it to build a property portfolio or invest in shares of other businesses. Therefore, a true assessment of the use of this capital in the business is to review the return that the investment has earned for the business owner and compare it to the return that they could have earned elsewhere.

If you invest £1 million in your business and generate £100,000 in net profits, you have received a 10% return. You then compare this against the return that you could have achieved deploying your money in other avenues. There are of course different risks associated with different investments and these need to be considered too.

Value is created when the return generated in a business is more than the cost of the capital.

The most important measures of return in a business are the return on invested capital (RoIC) and the return on equity (RoE). The RoIC measures the total return all capital providers to the business receive whereas the RoE measures the return that the equity shareholders receive. In this book, we will make some assumptions to simplify the definitions of income and assets and focus on understanding these concepts and using them practically.

> # Key Principle: A business creates value when its return is more than the cost of its capital

Return on assets (RoA)

The most important measure of the return to the debt and equity stakeholders in a business is the return on invested capital (RoIC):

$$RoIC = return \div invested\ capital$$

where

$$\text{Return} = \text{net operating income}$$
$$= \text{operating income after tax}$$

and

$$\text{Invested capital} = \text{total equity} + \text{external debt}$$

Net operating income is used as this reflects the total return after tax that all external capital providers receive. The denominator of the equation is therefore all external capital.

Taking a business's profit after tax, as seen in the P&L, and removing the effect of financial income and expense, we arrive at the net operating profit. On the balance sheet, if we consolidate all external providers of capital, all equity holders, long-term and short-term debt, we get the invested capital.

Neither of these numbers is usually presented clearly in financial accounts. For the sake of simplicity, the return on assets ratio (RoA) may be used. This can be derived directly from the P&L and Balance Sheet:

$$\text{Return on assets} = \text{return} \div \text{assets}$$

where

$$\text{Return} = \text{net operating income}$$

and

Assets = total assets − current liabilities
= total equity + long-term liabilities

As an example, if total assets were £3,251,500, current liabilities were £134,000 and net operating income was £430,000, RoA would be:

£430,000 ÷ (£3,251,000 − £134,000)
= £430,000 ÷ £3,117,500 = 13.8%

RoA can also be split to indicate the profitability and the efficiency of the business:

$$\frac{\text{Net operating income}}{\text{assets}}$$

$$= \frac{\text{net operating income}}{\text{turnover}} \times \frac{\text{turnover}}{\text{assets}}$$

Splitting RoA into its components begins to give real, actionable information to the management of the business.

Net operating income/turnover is the operating margin of the business and indicates its operating profitability. By increasing operating profitability management directly increases the business's RoA.

Turnover/assets (also called the asset turnover ratio) indicates the efficiency of the business. The more sales a business can generate on a fixed base of assets, the more efficient it is in its use of these assets. Increasing asset turnover through reducing the amount deployed in assets also directly increases the RoA of the business.

Therefore,

$$RoA = \text{operating margin} \times \text{asset turnover}$$

or

$$RoA = \text{profitability} \times \text{efficiency}$$

To take the previous example and add that business revenue was £2,000,000, this would translate to:

$$\text{Operating margin} = \text{net operating income} \div \text{revenue}$$
$$= £430,000 \div £2,000,000 = 21.5\%$$

and

$$\text{Asset turnover} = \text{turnover} \div \text{assets}$$
$$= £2,000,000 \div £3,117,500 = 0.64x$$

and

$$RoA = \text{operating margin} \times \text{asset turnover}$$
$$= 21.5\% \times 0.64x = 13.8\%$$

Looking at these numbers, we can see that the business runs at a good operating margin but has a lot of assets and scores low on efficiency of use of these assets. The overall RoA, therefore, is lower due to lower efficiency. This does not show how well the efficiency compares with other businesses in the industry in which the business operates, as different industries need different levels of assets to achieve their sales. Even so, it does give an indication of how a business needs both profitability and an efficient use of capital to generate returns.

Separating the RoA into its components, operating margin and asset turnover, also gives us an ability to look at the fundamentals of the business. Consider these businesses:

	RoA	=	Operating margin	×	Asset turnover
Business A	15%	=	30%	×	0.5
Business B	15%	=	7.5%	×	2.0

These two businesses, while generating the same return on assets, are fundamentally different. Business A is a high-margin business, potentially a Louis Vuitton in its industry, and Business B is a low-margin business, potentially a Zara in its industry. Business A sells a very profitable product but requires a lot of assets, perhaps in stores and machinery, to generate sales. Business B sells a much less profitable product and focuses on continuous movement of goods and high asset turnover.

From a return standpoint the two businesses are identical but the strategy and management required to run them are dramatically different. Neither business is objectively better than the other but, given how different they are, if they were part of the same group of businesses it would augur well for management to ensure that they are not run by a single team as the skills and decision-making required would be quite different.

This analysis is all the more important when looking to merge with another business in the industry. It is important to look at the fundamental numbers of the business, to decipher whether the businesses can be merged to generate value.

Key Principle: Operating margin and asset turnover both contribute to returns and together define the strategic positioning of the business

Return on equity (RoE)

Shareholders' equity is the difference between the business's total assets and its total liabilities.

Shareholders' equity has three sources. The first is the capital that was originally raised, perhaps by selling preferred and common stock to the public. The second is any later sales of preferred and common stock to the public once the business was up and running. The third, and most important to us, is the retained earnings that have accumulated in the business. Since all equity belongs to the business, and since the business belongs to the common shareholders, the equity really belongs to the common shareholders, which is why it is called shareholders' equity.

Now, if we are shareholders in a business, we would be interested in how good a job management does at allocating our money, so we can earn even more. If they are bad at it, we won't be happy and might even sell our shares and put our money elsewhere. But if they are really good at it, we might even buy more of the business, along with everyone else who is impressed with management's ability to put shareholders' equity to good and profitable use. To this end, the RoE equation indicates management's efficiency in allocating shareholders' money:

$$RoE = return \div total\ equity$$

where

$$Return = profit\ after\ tax.$$

As an example, if total equity was £468,500 and profit after tax was £197,000 RoE would be £197,000 ÷ £468,500 = 42%.

RoE can also be split to indicate the profitability and efficiency of the business and the effect of leverage in amplifying the returns it achieves. This analysis was formulated for the DuPont Corporation and bears its name.[8] It helps the equity holder understand where their return is coming from:

---

8   DuPont framework invented by DuPont salesman Donaldson Brown in 1912.

$$\frac{\text{Profit after tax}}{\text{Equity}} = \frac{\text{profit after tax}}{\text{turnover}} \times \frac{\text{turnover}}{\text{assets}} \times \frac{\text{assets}}{\text{equity}}$$

Profit after tax/turnover is the net margin of the business and indicates its overall profitability.

Turnover/assets is the asset turnover ratio, which we have just examined.

Assets/equity measures the financial leverage in the business. A business that has used high debt but relatively little equity to finance its assets has a higher 'leverage effect' on its RoE.

Therefore,

RoE = net margin × asset turnover × leverage

or

RoE = profitability × efficiency × leverage

Key Principle: A key driver of the return a business owner receives is the leverage in the business

To return to the example we looked at earlier in this chapter, we can understand RoE through its components as:

Net margin = profit after tax ÷ turnover
= £197,000 ÷ £2,000,000 = 9.85%

and

$$\text{Asset turnover} = \text{turnover} \div \text{assets}$$
$$= £2{,}000{,}000 \div £3{,}117{,}500 = 0.64\text{x}$$

and

$$\text{Leverage} = \text{assets} \div \text{equity}$$
$$= £3{,}117{,}500 \div £468{,}500 = 6.65\text{x}$$

and

$$\text{RoE} = \text{net margin} \times \text{asset turnover} \times \text{leverage}$$
$$= 9.85\% \times 0.64\text{x} \times 6.65\text{x} = 42\%$$

Looking at these numbers, we can see that the business runs at a low margin (driven by high interest costs) and has a lot of assets and scores low on how efficiently it uses these assets. But it has significant leverage to fund its assets and hence the overall RoE is quite good. This does not show whether the leverage is higher than or lower than the industry average, but the approach clearly appears to be working for the equity shareholders.

The breakdown of the RoE into its components gives an indication of how a business needs profitability, an efficient use of capital and leverage to generate returns.

This is a key metric because it indicates the return the owner of the equity receives for the investment they have made in the business. Few other avenues, apart from their own business, could boast returns of 42%. Given that a lot of this return is being driven by leverage, the business owner needs to recognise that they need to try and reduce debt-servicing costs while maintaining high leverage to continue to generate high returns for themselves.

Cost of equity

To measure the value the business creates for its owner(s), the RoE needs to be compared to the cost of that equity. As mentioned earlier, every business owner has a range of options for deploying their money (equity). The total equity (the original investment and the retained earnings of the business together) is the amount the business owner has chosen to invest in their business.

The RoE that the owner could reasonably expect if this investment had instead been deployed in a venture with the same risk profile as the business is referred to as the cost of equity.

A simple way of looking at this would be to work out what an external investor would expect in returns if they were to buy equity in the business. An investor would typically have multiple options to invest their funds – with varying risk profiles. For example, they might expect to get 2% interest on bank deposits (in 'normal' times, at any rate), 5% interest on debt investments, 8% return on property investments and 10% return investing in the stock market. You'll note that, as the risk of the investment increases, so too does the return expected.

A cost of equity of 12% implies that the investors in the business would expect a 12% return, to compensate for the risk of investing their equity in the business. Value is created when the RoE generated by the business is higher than the cost of equity. With a 42% return and a 12% cost, the business is creating value of a net 30% on all equity invested – and this is potentially a strong reason to keep reinvesting profits in the business to fund growth.

Cost of capital

To measure the value the business creates as an entity, we need to look at the total return it generates on all capital invested in it. In this case, the RoA needs to be compared to the cost of all the capital invested in the business.

Capital often comes from multiple sources, all with different risk profiles – debt is often cheaper and less risky for the provider than equity capital and therefore the expected return on it is also lower. The cost of capital is usually calculated as a weighted average of the varying costs of different types of capital.

For example, if the cost of equity is 12% and the equity is £468,500; and the interest cost is £146,000 on a debt of £2,629,000; the weighted average cost of capital (WACC) would be:

$$\text{WACC}$$

$$= (\text{cost of equity} \times \text{total equity}) + (\text{cost of debt} \times \text{total debt}) \div (\text{total equity} + \text{total debt})$$

$$= ((\text{cost of equity} \times \text{total equity}) + \text{interest cost}) \div (\text{total equity} + \text{total debt})$$

$$= ((£468,500 \times 12\%) + £146,000) \div (£468,500 + £2,629,000)$$

$$= £202,220 \div £3,097,500 = 6.53\%$$

With a cost of capital at 6.53%, value is created by the business when the RoA it generates is higher than the cost of capital. With a 13.8% RoA and a 6.53% cost of capital, the business is generating value of a net 7.27% on all capital invested – and this is potentially a strong reason both to keep reinvesting profits and to take on more debt to fund growth in the business.

Value creation

A fundamental principle in business is that value is created when the return generated on the investment is more than the cost of the investment.

Economic value added (EVA)[9] and economic profit (EP) are used to indicate the value that is being created by a business, through measuring the risk-adjusted profit it generates over and above what the capital could have earned if invested elsewhere. For example, with a WACC of 6.53% and a RoA of 13.8%, £3,117,500 of invested capital generates value calculated as:

$$\text{Value created} = (\text{RoIC} - \text{WACC}) \times \text{invested capital}$$
$$= (13.8\% - 6.53\%) \times £3,117,500 = 7.27\%$$
$$\times £3,117,500 = £226,642$$

A business focused on creating value will seek to do so through a combination of high returns on low capital investment and at the same time minimise the cost of capital by ensuring that the capital deployed in the business is sourced at as low a cost as is viable.

Once a business has increased value through combining these three strategies, the focus needs to change, to ensuring that higher value can be generated by investing more capital, while maintaining the value equation. This is the growth impetus for all value-creating businesses – growth in turnover, profitability, cash flow and also capital invested.

Key Principle: First ensure value is being created, then increase investment to grow the business

---

9   A term coined by Stern Value Management, 1983.

18
Leverage

A lever is a simple machine that allows us to gain mechanical advantage by increasing the amount of output achieved for the same amount of effort. When Archimedes said, 'Give me a lever long enough and a fulcrum on which to place it, and I shall move the world', he was referring to the power of a lever to significantly alter the effort and output equation.

The term leverage occurs in finance because of the multiple 'levers' that are present in a business to help it magnify its returns. Understanding how to apply the right financial and operating leverage in the business often helps unlock the real potential of the business for a lot less effort than would otherwise be required.

Increase in leverage is an increase in risk in the business and therefore operating and financial leverage need to be applied in a balanced manner, often setting one off against the other. If the business naturally has a lot of operating leverage, taking on financial leverage multiplies risk (along with potential returns) and needs to be approached with a good understanding of the current numbers and the potential of the business.

Using financial leverage to amplify returns

While financial leverage has been covered partially in Chapter 8, this chapter looks at how leverage in a business can dramatically amplify its RoE.

If debt is available at a certain rate of interest and the business is confident that it can make a rate of return higher than that, it makes sense to deploy debt to magnify the return. As an example, if the RoA is 13.8% and the business can raise debt at 4%, the difference between these two returns would flow directly to the equity holder, the business owner.

One way to understand the effect of leverage is to look at the balance sheet. Consider two different businesses with the same overall assets but different capital structures:

Business A

Total assets	£2,000,000	Total external debt	£500,000
		Total equity	£1,500,000
Total	£2,000,000	Total	£2,000,000

Business B

Total assets	£2,000,000	Total external debt	£1,500,000
		Total equity	£500,000
Total	£2,000,000	*Total*	£2,000,000

Assuming both businesses achieve an operating profit of £400,000 and pay interest on their debt at a rate of 10%, and assuming for simplicity that tax plays no part in the decision, both businesses have the same RoA, 10%.

However, for Business A:

$$\text{Net profit} = £400,000 - (10\% \times £500,000)$$
$$= £400,000 - £50,000 = £350,000$$

and therefore

$$\text{RoE} = £350,000 \div £1,500,000 = 23\%.$$

And for Business B

$$\text{Net profit} = £400,000 - (10\% \times £1,500,000)$$
$$= £400,000 - £150,000 = £250,000$$

and therefore

$$\text{RoE} = £250,000 \div £500,000 = 50\%.$$

Business B returns more than double what Business A returns to its shareholders.

More importantly, as each business grows through continuing to retain earnings, the effect of compounding returns makes Business B a significantly better business to invest in compared to Business A.

The caveat, of course, is that the business should be able to continue to meet both the interest payments and the capital repayments, while generating a RoA that is higher than what it is paying for its debt.

Given the dramatic increase in returns to shareholders through debt, it is incumbent upon every business owner and management team to seriously ask themselves whether they have chosen the best capital structure (combination of debt and equity) for their business.

Key Principle: Leverage amplifies expected returns by amplifying risk

When taking debt, it is important to look at the cash flows available, to be able to meet the interest charges and principal repayments on the debt on a regular basis and so avoid any defaults or breach any covenants that a lender may impose. As cash flow is usually not directly presented in the annual accounts of a business, lenders rely on a proxy for cash flow, the earnings before interest, tax, depreciation and amortisation (EBITDA). Two ratios that are often used for measuring leverage are the debt multiple and the interest cover ratio:

$$\text{Debt multiple} = \text{total debt} \div \text{EBITDA}$$

$$\text{Interest coverage ratio}$$
$$= (\text{EBITDA} + \text{other income}) \div \text{interest}$$

As an example, if:

Earnings	= £197,000
Tax	= £96,000
Interest	= £146,000
Depreciation	= £50,000
Amortisation	= £0
Other Income	= £9,000
Debt	= £2,649,000

then:

$$\text{EBITDA} = £197,000 + £96,000 + £146,000$$
$$+ £50,000 + £0 = £489,000$$

$$\text{Debt multiple} = £2,649,000 \div £489,000 = 5.42x$$

and

$$\text{Interest coverage} = (£489,000 + £9,000)$$
$$\div £146,000 = 3.41x$$

Usually, an interest cover ratio greater than three is seen as a sign of a healthy business whereas a ratio below two is considered a cause for concern. A debt multiple greater than three usually points to the business using too much debt. In the above example, in isolation, the debt multiple for the business indicates a high level of debt but interest coverage indicates that the debt is affordable and the company is able to cover the repayments on the high level of debt.

What having good credit means

The different RoE for businesses with and without debt indicates that where a business is creating value, debt is usually a good thing. Unfortunately, this is often in direct conflict with the objectives of lenders, who would rather lend to businesses with low or no debt.

Banks and lenders who the business approaches for loans will often apply initial and ongoing covenants, before deciding whether to accept the application and considering the interest rate they would like to charge and the security they would require. Some typical covenants used by lenders include:

Maximum debt multiple: net debt ÷ EBITDA

Minimum debt services coverage ratio (DSCR):

EBITDA ÷ total interest, or cash flow from operations (CFO) ÷ capital and interest repayments

Minimum liquidity ratios:

current assets ÷ current liabilities,
or cash ÷ current liabilities

Consider Businesses A and B again, through the lender's covenant lens. Both businesses have an operating profit of £430,000 and pay interest of 10% (and taxes are not considered, for simplicity). Business A therefore pays £50,000 in interest every year whereas Business B pays £150,000.

Business A

Interest	= £50,000
EBITDA	= £430,000
Net debt	= £500,000
Debt multiple	= £500,000 ÷ £430,000 = 1.16x
DSCR	= £430,000 ÷ £50,000 = 8.60x

Business B

Interest	= £150,000
EBITDA	= £430,000
Net debt	= £1,500,000
Debt multiple	= £1,500,000 ÷ £430,000 = 3.49x
DSCR	= £430,000 ÷ £150,000 = 2.87x

Comparing the two businesses:

	Business A	*Business B*
Debt multiple	1.16x	3.49x
DSCR	8.6x	2.87x

Business A has a much lower debt multiple and a much higher debt service coverage ratio and most banks would consider it a better credit risk than Business B.

We know from the previous section that Business B creates a lot more value for the business owner and this illustrates the varying interests underlying debt and equity. A management team that is not reviewing their business numbers is likely to be influenced by banks to reduce debt even though the debt may significantly enhance returns for them.

> \# *Key Principle: A lender's incentives are not always aligned with the business owner's incentives*

Operating leverage

All costs in the P&L can be classified into fixed and variable costs based on whether they vary with reasonable changes in production and sales (we say 'reasonable', because almost all costs may vary with large changes in sales).

Fixed costs are expenses that usually remain the same irrespective of how much the business produces and sells. Typical examples include rent and insurance.

Variable costs are expenses that are directly affected by how much a business produces and sells. Examples could be the raw material costs, distribution costs and sales commissions.

Sometimes, all expenses after the gross profit are pretty much fixed and the cost of sales is a good approximation of variable costs. But often there will be variable components of cost that are included in administrative expenses – sales commissions and bonuses, transportation costs and credit card charges are examples of such costs.

If a business chooses to employ people to deliver a service but is really billing its customers by the hour, it would be sensible to break down the salaries of the delivery team into variable and fixed components too.

This classification is not required for the purposes of financial accounts, but it does help management understand how much operating leverage they have and also how resistant to varying market conditions their business is. It may sometimes make sense, therefore, to reclassify and recategorise variable costs, and record them above the gross profit calculation, as part of the cost of sales, leaving the fixed costs below this line as part of the administrative expenses.

Operating leverage measures the leverage built into the operations of the business and reflects how changes in sales would impact its profitability. A high operating leverage means that small increases in sales would substantially increase profitability and, similarly, a small decrease in sales would substantially decrease profitability.

Operating leverage = fixed cost ÷ total costs
= fixed costs ÷ (fixed costs + variable costs)

Returning to Business A and Business B:

	Business A	Business B
Sales	£2,000,000	£2,000,000
Gross margin	60%	70%
Gross profit	£1,200,000	£1,400,000
Fixed cost	£770,000	£970,000
Operating profit	£430,000	£430,000
Variable costs	£800,000	£600,000
Operating leverage	$\dfrac{£770,000}{\left(£770,000 + £800,000\right)}$ = 0.49x	$\dfrac{£970,000}{\left(£970,000 + £600,000\right)}$ = 0.62x

Business B has lower variable costs and higher fixed costs, which could arise for example by having in-house sales teams on fixed salary rather than agency sales and distributors. The overall cost structures of the two businesses are similar but they have taken slightly different decisions on how to structure the costs in the business.

If the market and businesses are growing, a 10% growth in sales has very different results for the two businesses:

	Business A	Business B
Sales	£2,200,000	£2,200,000
Gross margin	60%	70%
Gross profit	£1,320,000	£1,540,000
Fixed cost	£770,000	£970,000
Operating profit	£550,000	£570,000
% increase	27.9%	32.6%

Business B's operating leverage means that a 10% increase in sales translates to a 32.6% increase in the operating profit, while for Business A the same increase in sales increases operating profit by 27.9%.

In a growth environment, therefore, it makes sense to increase operating leverage by replacing variable costs by fixed costs. For a business looking at years of growth ahead in a stable economic environment, management needs to evaluate cost allocation strategies – such as replacing sub-contractors with full-time staff – to increase the operating leverage in the business.

Equally, when times are tougher and sales are steady or declining, operating leverage needs to be decreased by replacing fixed costs with variable costs and management needs to evaluate strategies such as replacing fixed contracts with costs that can be directly linked to sales, to decrease the operating leverage in the business.

> *# Key Principle: Think higher fixed costs for*
> *steadily growing businesses and higher variable*
> *costs when the business outlook is less predictable*

Combined leverage analysis

An increase in leverage increases the variability of the returns of the business. As businesses can have both operating and financial leverage, it helps to monitor the combined effect in order to manage the associated impacts. This is done by combining the operating leverage and financial leverage into a single metric.

To calculate the combined leverage, operating leverage is measured as:

$$\text{Degree of operating leverage}$$
$$= (\text{sales} - \text{variable costs}) \div$$
$$(\text{sales} - \text{variable costs} - \text{fixed costs})$$

and financial leverage is measured as:

$$\text{Degree of financial leverage}$$
$$= (\text{sales} - \text{variable costs} - \text{fixed costs}) \div (\text{sales} -$$
$$\text{variable costs} - \text{fixed costs} - \text{interest expense})$$

Combined leverage is measured as:

$$\text{Combined leverage}$$
$$= \text{degree of operating leverage} \times \text{degree of}$$
$$\text{financial leverage}$$

$$= \frac{(\text{sales} - \text{variable costs}) \times (\text{sales} - \text{variable costs} - \text{fixed costs})}{(\text{sales} - \text{variable costs} - \text{fixed costs}) \times (\text{sales} - \text{variable costs} - \text{fixed costs} - \text{interest expense})}$$

$$= (\text{sales} - \text{variable costs}) \div (\text{sales} - \text{variable costs} - \text{fixed costs} - \text{interest expense})$$

Returning to Business A and Business B:

	Business A	Business B
Sales	£2,000,000	£2,000,000
Gross margin	60%	70%
Gross profit	£1,200,000	£1,400,000
Fixed cost	£770,000	£970,000
Operating profit	£430,000	£430,000
Variable costs	£800,000	£600,000
Interest costs	£50,000	£150,000
Net profit	£380,000	£280,000
Degree of operating leverage	$\frac{(£2,000 - £800)}{(£2,000 - £800 - £770)}$ = 2.8x	$\frac{(£2,000 - £600)}{(£2,000 - £600 - £970)}$ = 3.3x
Degree of financial leverage	$\frac{(£1,200 - £770)}{(£1,200 - £770 - £50)}$ = 1.1x	$\frac{(£1,400 - £970)}{(£1,400 - £970 - £150)}$ = 5.1x
Combined leverage	$\frac{(£1,200)}{(£1,200 - £770 - £50)}$ = 3.2x	$\frac{(£1,400)}{(£1,400 - £970 - £150)}$ = 5.0x

The degree of operating leverage gives us a positive or negative multiple of the operating profit for every unit increase or decrease in sales. A 1% change in sales will change profitability by 2.8% for Business A and 3.3% for Business B.

The combined leverage gives us a positive or negative multiple of the net profit for every unit increase or decrease in sales. A 1% change in sales will change profitability by 3.2% for Business A and 5.0% for Business B.

If the market and businesses are growing, a 10% growth in sales has quite different results for the two businesses:

	Business A	Business B
Sales	£2,200,000	£2,200,000
Operating profit	£550,000	£570,000
Interest costs	£50,000	£150,000
Net profit	£500,000	£420,000
% increase	31.6%	50.0%

Key Principle: Leverage is neither good nor bad. It can significantly enhance returns if used wisely alongside a scorecard.

19
Valuation

This chapter explores a few of the techniques commonly used to value a business. While a business has different values for different buyers, there are some recurring themes in the process of valuing a business which reflect how management could seek to increase the value of their business.

The first concept to be clear on is what is being valued. Is it the assets of the business? These could be the value they are recorded in the balance sheet at or their market value. Is the whole business being valued, or just a part of it? This brings in the concept of goodwill: some buyers may be willing to pay a premium for the business. Are you putting a figure on the value to the business owner? This is the value of the equity held in the business.

Looking at the balance sheet of the business, we can arrive at a total assets figure, which is the sum of the non-current and current assets and is sometimes referred to as the book value of the business.

Non-current assets	Current liabilities
Current assets	Non-current liabilities
	Total equity

If we add to this any assets and liabilities that the business does not declare on its balance sheet (for example, property or equipment which is on a long-term contracted lease or goodwill and brand value associated with the business which has not been included in the accounts), we get a slightly more representative picture of the book value or total asset value of the business.

Non-current assets	Current liabilities
Current assets	Non-current liabilities
	Total equity
Off-balance sheet assets	Off-balance sheet liabilities

However, as we know, the book value is based on historical cost (cost at the time of purchase) and on the business's depreciation strategy, and the current market value might be higher or lower than this. Nor does it consider expected future growth or the goodwill of the business. If you wish to incorporate this, the value of the business can be represented as follows:

Non-current assets	Current liabilities
Current assets	Non-current liabilities
	Total equity
Off-balance sheet assets	Off-balance sheet liabilities
Growth assets	Market value adjustments (MVA)

The value thus represented is termed the aggregate or enterprise value (EV) of the business. It is the value available to all the providers of capital to the business. If we remove from this the value of the debt in the business, we arrive at the business's equity value or the value available to the shareholders or business owners.

As an example, the value of a house on mortgage is the EV and the owner's equity in the house is the EV less the outstanding mortgage.

> # *Key Principle: Enterprise value (EV) = equity value + debt*

The two most common approaches to valuation are discounted cash flow (DCF) and relative valuation.

Discounted cash flow

DCF assumes that the value of the business is based entirely on the future cash flows that it can generate. These estimated cash flows must be discounted to the present, using a risk-weighted discount rate to arrive at the value of the business.

To put it simply, three things determine the value of a business: cash flows, growth and risk.

If the business is expected to generate free cash flow of CF_1 at the end of the first year, CF_2 at the end of the second year and so on for 'n' years and the risk associated with the cash flows is 'r', the DCF approach posits that the value of the business is:

$$\frac{CF_1}{(1+r)_1} + \frac{CF_2}{(1+r)_2} + \frac{CF_3}{(1+r)_3} + ...+ \frac{CF_n}{(1+r)_n}$$

This can be further modified by detailing the components of each year's cash flow and varying assumptions: the growth rate, the life of the business and the risk discount.

Depending on which cash flows and which discount rate are used DCF can be used to arrive at both the EV and the equity value.

Given the complexity and detailed estimation required in DCF, most small or medium-sized enterprises (SME) are bought and sold on relative valuation metrics which could be considered a simplified form of DCF.

Relative valuation

Relative valuation approaches compare the values of other, similar businesses to arrive at a valuation of your business.

The idea of relative valuation is that we can find comparable businesses, choose some financial metrics to standardise the comparison and establish a relative value for your business by comparing its metrics with those of these comparable businesses. The most popular variables used to standardise valuation are earnings and EBITDA (see Chapters 4 and 18).

The most popular of the relative valuation standardised metrics are the price/ earnings (P/E) ratio and the EV/EBITDA ratio.

The P/E ratio is a metric used to compare shares traded on stock exchanges; P refers to the current market price of shares in a business and E is a ratio: earnings per share. Where a business is not traded on a stock exchange, P/E can still be established, though with a slightly different methodology where P refers to the total equity value of the business (preferably, what a buyer offers to buy the equity) and E is the business's profit after tax.

The EV/EBITDA ratio is often applied to businesses being acquired, and EV is the sum of the debt and the market value of the business's equity. EBITDA refers to the cash earnings available to the business before interest and tax obligations; EBITDA is used as a proxy for operating cash generated by the business.

Both the P/E and EV/EBITDA ratios derive from DCF valuation. The P/E ratio assumes the earnings of the business are a close proxy for the cash flow available to the business owner and calculates the value of the business to the business owner. The EV/EBITDA ratio assumes the EBITDA of the business is a close proxy for the cash flow available to all capital providers to the business and calculates an enterprise value as described above.

 # Key Principle: Relative valuation is simplified DCF

As an example, if the equity of a business has been sold for £3 million, it had debts of £3 million, its earnings were £300,000 and its EBITDA was £700,000, the P/E ratio of that business is:

$$£3 \text{ million} \div £300,000 = 10\text{x}$$

and the EV/EBITDA ratio of that business is:

$$£6 \text{ million} \div £700,000 = 8.57\text{x}$$

One interpretation of the 10x P/E ratio is that if the business is only expected to grow at the risk return rate (i.e. not create any value), the new business owner has effectively decided to pay the next ten years' business earnings to the previous owner. If the business grows faster than this, the amount paid will be earned back sooner. The growth rate assumptions, which would have been explicit in DCF calculations, are implied in relative valuation.

Similarly, an EV/EBITDA ratio of 8.57x implies that, if the business only grows at the risk-adjusted rate of return, the buying stakeholders have paid 8.57 years' EBITDA to the selling stakeholders...

Now, if we are valuing a business similar to the one above and have this information for that business:

Earnings	= £197,000
Tax	= £96,000
Interest	= £146,000
Depreciation	= £50,000
Amortisation	= £0
Debt	= £2,649,000

we can put a value on the business, using the EV/EBITDA multiple, as follows:

$$EV = EBITDA \times 8.57$$
$$= (£197,000 + £96,000 + £146,000 + £50,000 + £0)$$
$$\times 8.57$$
$$= £489,000 \times 8.57 = £4,191,000$$

Given the debt is £2,649,000, the value to the business owner is £4,191,000 − £2,649,000 = £1,542,000.

We can also calculate the value to the business owner directly using the P/E multiple, as earnings × 10 = £197,000 × 10 = £1,970,000.

The two relative valuation metrics have provided different valuations. Valuation is an art because of the underlying assumptions, and it is therefore usually a good idea to use multiple valuation metrics to arrive at a range of valuation.

The two valuation errors that kill deals

Business purchases in the SME sector are often assumed to be 'cash free, debt free' because in this special case the EV and the equity value are the same. Once a valuation has been agreed between the buyer and seller, both parties may agree to leave in the business all debt or cash the business has and adjust the value payable to the seller accordingly.

The first error unsophisticated sellers often make is to assume that the value of the business and the value of their stake in the business are the same. If the business is funded mostly by debt, the value to the business owner is likely to be a lot lower than the EV they have arrived at. Equally, if the business has been storing surplus cash that is not used for its operations, its value to the owner is likely to be more than the EV based on relative valuation.

If a business is valued at £10 million with £8 million of debt, and you want to take a 50% stake in it, what should your investment be? A rapacious seller may try to sell a stake in their business based on EV rather than equity value. All else being equal, in this scenario a 50% equity stake in the business has a value of £1 million.

A second error unsophisticated sellers often make is to assume that once EV has reached a certain multiple of EBITDA, their stock and net working capital need to be added to this figure to arrive at the value of the business.

This is a misunderstanding of how relative valuation works and the result it arrives at. The EV/EBITDA ratio assumes that all assets that the business requires to generate the EBITDA have been taken into account. Paying separately for working capital is double counting.

Key Principle: Multiple × EBITDA = EV; understand both sides of the equation

20

Increasing The Value Of A Business

Fundamentally, the value of a business is based on cash being generated, expected growth of cash flow and the risk associated with future cash flows. These three variables tell us everything we need to know, to understand how we could improve the value of a business.

This is again a simplified way of looking at DCF. Looking back at the base DCF calculation:

$$\frac{CF_1}{(1+r)_1} + \frac{CF_2}{(1+r)_2} + \frac{CF_3}{(1+r)_3} + ... + \frac{CF_n}{(1+r)_n}$$

if the cash flow in each period grows at the same growth rate, 'g', then:

$$CF_n = CF_{(n-1)} \times (1 + g)$$

If we also assume that the cash flow continues to grow in perpetuity, the DCF calculation simplifies to:

$$\frac{CF_1}{(r-g)}$$

This equation therefore identifies three key variables that impact the business's value.

Improving cash generation

A business with strong operating profitability and consistent cash flow is likely to be valued higher than one which does not have these defining characteristics.

To improve its ability to generate cash, the business needs to put in place processes to consistently and accurately measure operating profitability and also how operating profits and cash move, to ensure that there are no diversions and leakages of cash and that cash flow remains consistent.

Next, management needs to focus on consistently maintaining and increasing operating profitability with decision-making focused on the bottom line of the business.

You also need to explore how the business could create and build recurring revenue streams to allow it to achieve consistency of revenue and therefore cash. If the business does not already have ongoing contracts and subscriptions that keep its customers coming back again and again, it needs to consider how it could change its value proposition to allow for recurring revenue and returning customers.

Decreasing risk associated with cash flows

A business with a competitive advantage is usually one which has a differentiated product and service and has used this to create a moat around itself which competitors cannot cross. You need to start asking how you can differentiate your business from the competition.

Documenting all systems and creating operating manuals can demonstrate that the risk of operational mishaps has been minimised. Similarly, building a second tier of management decreases dependency on the owner and therefore the risk of cash flow being interrupted.

A concentration of business with a few customers or with a few suppliers or employees is also a risk factor which needs to be addressed to increase the value of the business.

Increasing potential growth

As the business's customer base grows, it needs to consistently gather customer feedback and work to improve products and services based on this feedback. This ensures customer satisfaction can be improved, with customers continuing to come back and grow the business. It also reduces the risk associated with the company's cash flows as repeat customers bring more stability to ongoing cash flows.

Growth opportunities across new geographies, products and markets, and opportunities for synergies with other businesses, open growth potential for the business. Inorganic growth through strategic acquisitions becomes another avenue where capital can be deployed to pursue growth.

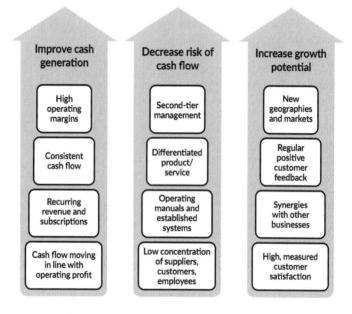

Improving the value of the business

Conclusion

A strong understanding of the language of numbers gives you an ability to dive deep into the fundamentals of your business.

If we now go back to the problem Roger was facing in Chapter 1, we can use our knowledge of financial statements to understand the root causes of the problem and implement the right solutions.

CASE STUDY: Roger's business

The immediate issue Roger was facing was one of cash flow. We know now that cash flow comes from three sources – operations, investment and financing. Reviewing the numbers, we realised that while the business was making profit, cash flow from operations was not increasing as the profits were stuck in the cash conversion cycle.

This is the first problem we decided to tackle alongside Roger.

We estimated the cost of funds that the business could borrow and decided to offer customers an early payment incentive that was less than the cost of funds. Quite a few customers took up the offer and paid down the receivables. The receivable days in the business decreased from ninety-one to fifty, releasing around £500,000 of cash into the business.

Roger was a fast payer – his suppliers loved that he would pay the moment their invoice reached him. This unfortunately had an effect on the business cash flow. He implemented a policy of paying all invoices on the due date and not before, and a cash flow forecast that ensured there was always cash available to meet payments falling due. Payable days increased from twelve to thirty, releasing a further £150,000 of cash into the business.

We implemented a system of regular stock takes measured alongside project timeline requirements to ensure that stock was only held for the minimum period required. Inventory days decreased from forty-nine to thirty, releasing another £150,000 of cash into the business.

Within a year Roger's cash conversion cycle, which had previously hovered around 128 days, dropped to 50 days, releasing £800,000 of cash into the business!

With the immediate problem of cash resolved, we started looking through the return metrics of the business.

Roger's business had an operating margin of 20% and an asset turnover of 0.5x, resulting in a RoA of 10%.

To improve the profitability of the business, we reviewed all costs and the pricing strategy of the business. We found that marketing spend had been growing over recent years. But there was no measure of the return this marketing was generating. As we mapped out where business was coming from, we realised that trade shows and sponsorships, a big part of the marketing budget, were in fact the least effective channels whereas social media-based advertising was bringing most of the new customers to the business. He stopped spending on non-productive marketing and redirected some of the budget to channels that were working.

While Roger was pricing on a mark-up basis, he was also consistently measuring gross margin. An extremely high conversion rate indicated that the pricing he was arriving at was positioning his business as a low-price player rather than a high-quality business. Further, the team would agree to all projects, irrespective of their size, whereas Roger was clear that the work involved in different projects was similar irrespective of their size and profitability. We decided to implement a guide to the minimum project size and also differentiated pricing. This immediately meant that several new estimates came out higher which, without losing much business, directly increased the operating margin of the business, to 27%.

We also decided to close down the business's least productive showrooms, to further decrease the capital employed in the business, increasing asset turnover to 0.65x.

With all of these changes, the business RoA increased to 27% × 0.65 = 17.55%.

We now reviewed the return that Roger himself was getting from the business. With a RoA significantly higher than the cost of funds, we knew that more leverage in the business would significantly increase the RoE. Roger had always avoided leverage but understood the amplifying affect it could have on the business. He established a target leverage ratio and raised a bank loan to help the business scale even faster.

The business increased leverage from 1.11x to 1.55x and RoE more than doubled from 11% to 27% × 0.65 × 1.55 = 27.20%.

In under a year of working with us, Roger's business continued to grow in double digits, but now he always had cash in the bank with a steadily increasing cash flow from operations and his RoE (and at the same time, valuation) more than doubled.

Winning scorecards

The improvements that come from understanding financial statements, though significant, are only part of the answer. They solve immediate problems and make the business healthier and more profitable. Remember, that what we really want to achieve is sustainable profitability. This is where having regular scorecards to look at makes a difference.

We worked with Roger to build a few different score-cards for his business:

The Profitability Scorecard

	Last week	This week	YTD target	YTD actual
Sales (£)				
Sales per job				
Break-even sales				
Gross profit (£)				
Gross margin %				

The Cash Flow Scorecard

	Target	Actual
Inventory days		
Receivable days		
Payable days		
Cash conversion period		
Cash balance		

The Operating Performance Scorecard

	Target	Actual
Operating profit (£)		
Operating profit %		
Operating profit per person		
Asset turnover (efficiency)		
Return on assets %		

The Equity Performance Scorecard

	Target	Actual
Net margin % (profitability)		
Asset turnover (efficiency)		
Leverage		
Return on equity %		

Roger had really become a scoring champion. He now knew how every component of his business was measured and what the score was at every point in time.

High and increasing cash flow from operations and RoE, and strong internal systems for measurement, meant that he had also increased the valuation multiple and therefore the valuation of his business significantly.

As lifetime students of business understand, it is not just the score but the learning each score gives that allows your business to optimise performance and deploy all available resources – including your time and effort – to win!

The Authors

Amol Maheshwari is a managing partner in Growth Idea, the UK's leading SME business coaching and consulting company. He is on the board of the Language Services Group, the UK's largest provider of foreign-language training to companies and government organisations and Actors in Industry, a leading roleplay-based training and coaching business. He also leads the private equity arm of S J Mann Solutions, a London-based investment business.

Amol has previously worked across investment banking and corporate finance, first with HSBC and then with Morgan Stanley. He has taught hundreds of students and management professionals fundamental financial concepts, business finance, valuation and financial modelling and has been a visiting faculty member at the Cranfield School of Management.

Amol is a High-Performance Executive (HPEX) board-certified consultant, a CFA charter holder and he has an MBA from the Indian Institute of Management, Bengaluru (Bangalore).

As part of Growth Idea's consulting arm, he has worked to help over a hundred businesses grow their profitability and strengthen each aspect of their business to achieve a higher valuation. The HPEX programme he delivers has been recognised as one of the top management development programmes in the world.

Shweta Jhajharia is a serial entrepreneur, an international business speaker and a leading global business consultant. Founder of Growth Idea, Shweta has personally worked with hundreds of businesses and has delivered over 15,000 hours of business coaching.

She has won many awards, including two prestigious International Stevie awards and the British Franchise Association's Judges Award, and has been featured by hundreds of media outlets including the BBC, *FT Adviser*, City AM, *Training Journal*, the *Evening Standard* and *Management Today*. She has consistently been ranked in the world's top thirty business coaching professionals.

Her book, *Sparks: Ideas to ignite your business growth* (Panoma Press, 2017) is an Amazon bestseller that draws on tested and proven strategies and stories to offer powerful ideas for sustainable double-digit growth in businesses.

Before turning to entrepreneurship, Shweta was Global Marketing Manager at Unilever. She has an MBA from the Indian Institute of Management, Bengaluru (Bangalore).

Find out more about Growth Idea at

🌐 www.growthidea.co.uk.